BIRDS BY COLOUR
The <u>Simplest</u> Identification Guide

MIKE LAMBERT
Illustrations by Alan Pearson

BLANDFORD

Other books by Mike Lambert and Alan Pearson

An Instant Guide to Birds 1985, USA; reprinted 1985, 1986, 1987, 1988, 1989, 1990.

Oiseaux 1988, France; reprinted 1989, 1990, 1991.

Pa Aderyn? 1988, Wales.

An Instant Guide to Freshwater Birds 1989, USA.

An Instant Guide to Seabirds 1989, USA.

An Instant Guide to Owls & Birds of Prey 1989, USA.

Letts Pocket Guide to Birds 1990, UK.

Dedicated to my parents and grandparents, whose knowledge was slight but enthusiastic, and who provided the impetus for my own interest in the subject. To my wife Barbara, and my children Jennie and Mark, for tolerating my long retreats while 'creating'. But especially to Madelaine Lunn, without whose persistence and belief I would never have lifted the pen in the first place.

A BLANDFORD BOOK

First published in the UK 1992
by Blandford
(a Cassell imprint)
Villiers House
41/47 Strand
London WC2N 5JE

Distributed in the United States
by Sterling Publishing Co., Inc.
387 Park Avenue South, New York, NY 10017–8810

Distributed in Australia
by Capricorn Link (Australia) Pty Ltd
P.O. Box 665, Lane Cove, NSW 2066

British Library Cataloguing-in-Publication Data
A catalogue record for this book is available from the British Library

ISBN 0–7137–2295–9

Typeset in Monophoto Helvetica by August Filmsetting, Haydock, St Helens
Printed in Great Britain by Bath Press Colourbooks, Glasgow

CONTENTS

ABOUT THE BRITISH TRUST FOR CONSERVATION VOLUNTEERS

BTCV is the country's leading charity protecting the environment by practical action.

For over thirty years the British Trust for Conservation Volunteers has been providing opportunities for individuals to turn their concern for the natural environment into positive action. Whether it is the conservation of nature care for the landscape or the greening of our towns or cities, BTCV offers people of all ages and backgrounds the challenge to make their contribution.

In helping people meet this challenge BTCV needs to make nature and the environment more accessible to everyone – which is exactly what this excellent book does. Much of natural history is shrouded in long names and terminology which make it difficult for most of us to enjoy it. This book goes a long way to de-mystifying birdwatching for us. With this book, I believe, anyone can identify the birds they see on holiday, on their local walks or while they are undertaking conservation projects with BTCV.

For this reason, I have no hestiation in recommending this book to you; I hope you enjoy using it.

For more information about the work of BTCV write to the Information Officer:
BTCV
36 St Mary's Street
Wallingford
Oxfordshire OX1 0EU

Mike King, Divisional Director
May 1991

INTRODUCTION

Bird recognition is not always easy. Experienced bird people may use several key observations to obtain positive identifications. They usually already have a good enough knowledge to place an unknown bird in the right family group, e.g. it is one of the thrushes, or it is one of the gulls. This is clearly an advantage as it eliminates most of the 'impossible' species, and brings them to a few pages of probable candidates. Most bird recognition guides are very useful once the user has built up this previous knowledge.

However, beginners do not have this experience to build on.

Experience also teaches the value of observing posture, body proportions, flight patterns and habitats. Silhouettes can frequently be completely distinctive. But again, this all depends on some existing bank of prior knowledge, gained through experience.

So what is the answer?

The answer has been found by listening to beginners and inexperienced watchers trying to describe an unfamiliar bird. Invariably, the novice observer latches on to plumage colours and bird size (usually in relation to something more familiar e.g. a sparrow or pigeon). But with a few notable exceptions, the available guides still stick rigidly to scientific classification.

That's all very well, but I think we can do better.

What is required is to group together Britain and Ireland's (referred to as 'the region') commonest birds according to **observed colours**. This eliminates possible confusion with rarities that most people are unlikely to encounter in a lifetime of normal sightings. These observed colours can be either large areas of colour, e.g. the white on a gull, or specific colour markings – perhaps just a bar or patch of colour on a wing, e.g. the brilliant blue flash on a Jay's wing.

If a particular bird exhibits several noticeable colours, perhaps the colours blue and green, black, white and yellow on a Great Tit, then that bird must appear in each colour grouping. In this book it does – the Great Tit is included in all those colour sections. So it does not matter which colour strikes the observer as noticeable, the bird will be listed in whatever colour section he or she felt was prominent.

All that remains is to sequence all the birds in each colour section. This is achieved by listing them in increasing size order within the section, with a familiar species mentioned for comparison. Brief notes accompany each illustration to ensure the quickest possible exact identification.

The other major benefit of this approach is that males and females, juveniles and immatures, summer and winter plumages, are individually represented with a separate illustration wherever they are significantly different from each other. This means that the reader can successfully recognize a female Bullfinch for example, without having prior knowledge of what a male Bullfinch looks like! This is probably most useful with male and female ducks.

In addition, some domesticated birds and strains are included in this book. Novices repeatedly wonder why town pigeons do not appear in existing field guides, when they see them in every city centre. Likewise, the ugly Muscovy Duck is endlessly familiar at village ponds and at farms. These and several other distinctive varieties are included with appropriate explanatory notes.

This is a 'user-friendly' bird guide. No other identification guide uses this approach. If it sounds an easy method, there is a good reason. **It is!**

However, there may come a point when many readers will wish to gain more structured knowledge about birds. That is natural and to be encouraged. When you reach that stage (or, should you start to see species not included in this guide) then that will be the time to progress on to more specialist reference works. Some suggestions are listed at the end of this book.

Good watching!

Mike Lambert, Surrey, UK

HOW TO USE THIS BOOK

This book is divided into six colour sections.

The first four are **basic** colours. They are dull background colours which make up the majority of plumages. Each is often the most visible colour simply because there is a lot of it. They are **brown, white, grey** and **black**.

Then there are the **bright** colours. Mostly these appear as flashes or patches of colour (there are, of course, obvious exceptions, the Kingfisher for one), but they are often very visible and very good identification aids. **Yellow, orange** and **red** (including **pink**, of course) are grouped together in one section as they often intergrade anyway. Likewise **green** and **blue** are given a joint section.

Inclusions in a colour section may be subjective, and not every single colour on a bird is allowed for (if only for space considerations), but all significant areas of colour that will aid identification are included. Tones or shades of colour are given, e.g. 'very dark grey', 'chestnut-red', or 'olive-green'.

Let us suppose that you have just seen a bird with which you are unfamiliar. Unless the conditions are extreme, you will automatically have made certain key observations. These might be that:
(a) It was brownish, and that it showed a flash of yellow in its tail and wings when it flew and
(b) It was about the size of a sparrow.*

This information would be inadequate to expect rapid identification with traditional guides. However, it may well be sufficient with this one!

Use the size information at the top of the page in the colour section of your choice (allow a small margin either side, just in case of some error in assessing size), and you will find that there will probably be only a few possible candidates. There may only be one. If more colours were observed, the fact that the same bird appears in more than one colour section is even more likely to single out the correct species.

For 'proof positive' identification, start to look at the notes that accompany each illustration.

The top line gives the correct name of the bird, its size, and its residential status. Check the Glossary of Terms if you are unfamiliar with the categories shown for residential status, as it might be important. For instance, it will not be possible to see a Nightingale in this region in January; it is a summer visitor only.

The first paragraph shows where your chosen colour is located on the bird. This paragraph can be very helpful in itself if you are lucky enough to have prolonged views.

The second paragraph provides the Key Identification Features, and has an **eye symbol** 👁 alongside it. If you can still see the bird and those features are visible e.g. the 'cobalt-blue crown' on a Blue Tit, *then you have definitely identified the bird correctly.* If the key features are NOT there, then you have the WRONG bird, and must look at neighbouring illustrations. Remember, ALL the birds you are ever likely to see in a lifetime of normal watching are included.

The third and largest paragraph gives additional useful information and is indicated with a **star symbol** ★. This information may be broken down as follows:

(a) Some idea of common-ness is always given. You should not expect to see scarce birds in your garden repeatedly!

(b) Habitat – the most usual types of location are indicated (e.g. heathland, woodland), and so are any geographical variations (e.g. 'absent from Ireland', or 'restricted to Scottish coniferous forests').

(c) Confusion species – if there is another bird species which is similar, it is referred to in this paragraph, together with key features which will distinguish it from your bird.

(d) Finally, there may be some particular idiosyncrasy typical of your bird, such as the 'football-shaped' nest built by a Magpie, or the 'explosive take-off' of a Snipe.

It is as simple as that. If you follow this straightforward procedure, *you will find that this is bird-watching made easy!*

*By the way, your bird was a female or juvenile Greenfinch!

PARTS OF A BIRD

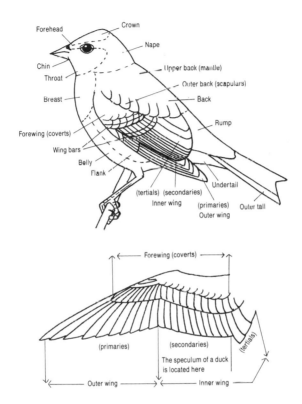

Forehead
Crown
Nape
Chin
Throat
Upper back (mantle)
Outer back (scapulars)
Breast
Back
Rump
Forewing (coverts)
Wing bars
Belly
Flank
Undertail
(tertials) (secondaries)
Inner wing
(primaries) Outer tail
Outer wing

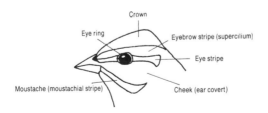

Forewing (coverts)

(primaries)

(secondaries)

(tertials)

The speculum of a duck
is located here

Outer wing

Inner wing

Crown
Eye ring
Eyebrow stripe (supercilium)
Eye stripe
Moustache (moustachial stripe)
Cheek (ear covert)

WREN   4 in (10 cm) resident

Virtually all brown.

👁 Tiny brown bird, with a cocked tail.

★ One of the most widespread and abundant birds in the region, found in almost any low cover. Whirring flight and amazingly loud song are both distinctive.

WILLOW WARBLER   4½ in (11 cm) summer visitor

Greenish brown upperparts and tail.

👁 'Clean' colours, no wing bar. Best identified by descending notes in song.

★ Abundant visitor. Widespread, found in any habitat with some ground cover. The Chiffchaff is similar but its 'dirtier' markings and 'chiff-chaff' song should separate them.

CHIFFCHAFF   4½ in (11 cm) summer visitor

Greenish brown upperparts and tail. 'Dirty' brownish tinge overall.

👁 'Dirty' colours, no wing bar. Song distinctive, two-note 'chiff-chaff'.

★ Very common, except in far north, requiring trees or scrub. Willow Warbler is similar, but its 'cleaner' markings and descending notes in song should separate them.

CRESTED TIT   4½ in (11 cm) resident

Back, upperwings and tail are a plain brown.

👁 Obvious black and white crest.

★ In Britain they are located only in coniferous forests of northern Scotland, where they are locally common. Possible confusion with black-capped Coal Tit.

MARSH TIT   4½ (11 cm) resident

Back, upperwings and tail are a plain brown.

👁 Glossy black cap, no wing bars or patches, and often-used 'pitchu' call.

★ Fairly common woodland species, restricted mainly to England and Wales. Willow Tit is very similar, but has a pale wing patch and gives 'eee' calls.

WILLOW TIT 4½ in (11 cm) resident

Back, upperwings and tail are a plain brown. But note paler wing patch.

👁 Dull black cap, pale wing patch, main call a sequence of 'eee's.

★ Fairly uncommon woodland species, breeding mainly in England and Wales. Marsh Tit is very similar, but has unmarked wings and gives 'pitchu' call.

GOLDFINCH adult 4¾ in (12 cm) resident

Mid-brown back. Flanks and breast markings are a warmer tone.

👁 Red, white and black head pattern.

★ Common and widespread (except in north Scotland), found on both open ground and in gardens. They love thistle seeds. Head pattern eliminates confusion with other species.

GOLDFINCH juvenile 4¾ in (12 cm) resident

Streaked brown head, back and breast.

👁 Single broad, brilliant yellow wing bars, with the head streaked brown.

★ Common and widespread (except in north Scotland), found on both open ground and in gardens. They love thistle seeds. The Siskin is similar, but shows double yellow wing bars and is clearly greenish.

SAND MARTIN 4¾ in (12 cm) summer visitor

All upperparts and breast bar are a plain brown.

👁 Swallow-type bird with brown breast bar.

★ Common and widespread, but declining. Requires banks or cliffs for nest burrow, usually in open country near water. May be confused with black and white House Martin, which has white rump and no breast bar.

REDPOLL male (both adults similar) 5 in (13 cm) resident

Streaked brown upperparts, with rump and flanks paler. Plain wings darker.

👁 Crimson forehead and black chin.

★ Reasonably common, but easy to miss. Often in large acrobatic flocks, they require trees, from heaths to conifer plantations. The adult male Linnet has a crimson forehead with a whitish chin.

SIZE: **WREN ↔ HOUSE SPARROW**

TREECREEPER   5 in (13 cm) resident

The upperparts are brown, streaked with buff. Buff wing bar.

👁 Tree-climbing behaviour (always upwards). Downcurved bill.

★ Associated exclusively with trees, mainly mature deciduous. Numerous and widespread, with no look-alikes. Actions and general appearance give rise to its description as 'mouse-like'.

SEDGE WARBLER   5 in (13 cm) summer visitor

All upperparts are brown, with crown and back bearing darker streaking.

👁 Very prominent whitish stripe over eye, with a black-streaked crown.

★ Common in reeds and other thick cover near water. Notable for loud churring song. Widespread across British Isles all summer. Compare Reed Warbler's plain plumage and faint eye stripe.

DARTFORD WARBLER   5 in (13 cm) resident

Very dark brown upperparts (with the head more of a dark grey).

👁 Underparts are a dark wine-red. Long tail is often cocked.

★ Very uncommon, only a few hundred birds being found in gorse-covered areas of southern England. Really a Mediterranean species, this is the very northern tip of its range.

REED WARBLER   5 in (13 cm) summer visitor

All upperparts are a plain, rather reddish brown.

👁 Uniformly plain, reddish brown upperparts. A bird of reed beds.

★ Reasonably common in southern English reed beds. Female Whitethroat and chubby Garden Warbler are similar, but both prefer drier hedgerow and woodland habitat. Other similar warblers all show streaked plumage.

WHINCHAT   5 in (13 cm) summer visitor

All upperparts are brown, bearing dark streaks and 'scalloping'.

👁 White eye stripe and border to cheek. Female duller than the male.

★ An open country species, locally common. Has favourite prominent perching places. Stonechat is quite similar, can occupy same habitat, but completely lacks the eye stripe.

STONECHAT   male 5 in (13 cm) resident

Very dark brown back and tail, with variable amounts of streaking visible.

👁 Entirely black head with prominent white neck patch.

★ Widely present, but with a markedly western distribution. A bird of open country, frequently seen atop a gorse bush. Female and juvenile are duller and more streaked, as is Whinchat.

STONECHAT   female and juvenile 5 in (13 cm) resident

Head and upperparts are brown. Crown to lower back is heavily streaked.

👁 Streaked head and upperparts, small white wing patch.

★ Widely present, but markedly western distribution. A bird of open country, often atop a gorse bush. Male has prominent white neck patch. Whinchat has white edging at base of tail.

PIED FLYCATCHER   female 5 in (13 cm) summer visitor

Most of head, upperparts and tail are a plain light brown.

👁 Brown and white plumage only, with clear white wing bar.

★ An uncommon visitor, exclusively associated with woodland, usually deciduous (mostly in Wales). Compare with Spotted Flycatcher (no wing bar), and female Chaffinch (double wing bar).

LITTLE STINT   juvenile 5 in (13 cm) passage migrant

Most of head and upperparts are brown. Back 'scalloped', two 'V'-markings.

👁 Tiny (smallest wader in the region), with a short, straight bill.

★ Rather uncommon, seen mainly on autumn passage, usually by inland water. Beware superficial resemblance to juvenile Dunlin (twice as bulky, longer downcurved bill).

LINNET   male 5½ in (13.5 cm) resident

Reddish brown back and forewings.

👁 Crimson forehead and breast, in summer. White on wings and tail, all seasons.

★ Widespread and numerous in most open country habitats. Forms twittering flocks outside the breeding season. Redpoll has black chin; Chaffinch has double white wing bars.

LINNET   female and juvenile 5¼ in (13.5 cm) resident

Brown head, upperparts and breast. Quite heavily streaked.

👁 White patches on wings and tail are very visible in flight.

★ Widespread and numerous in most open country habitats. Forms twittering flocks outside the breeding season. Redpoll lacks wing patches, and Chaffinch has double wing bars.

LESSER WHITETHROAT   5½ in (14 cm) summer visitor

Grey back has brownish tinge. Wings and tail are darker and browner.

👁 Dark grey mask, grey-brown back.

★ A scarce summer visitor, mostly found in south and east. Skulks in trees and scrub. Whitethroat has more reddish brown back, but beware faint mask on male. Garden Warbler is chubbier.

WHITETHROAT   male 5½ in (14 cm) summer visitor

All upperparts are a plain, rather reddish brown, except for grey head.

👁 Grey cap, white throat, and reddish brown back and wings.

★ A common summer visitor to scrubby locations. Female is brown-capped. Lesser Whitethroat is greyish above, with an obvious mask, and Garden Warbler is rather grey-throated.

WHITETHROAT   female and juvenile 5½ in (14 cm) summer visitor

All upperparts are a plain, rather reddish brown, including head.

👁 Reddish brown cap, back and wings. White throat. Prefers dry scrubby habitat.

★ A common summer visitor to scrubby locations. Male is grey-capped. Reed Warbler prefers wet locations. Lesser Whitethroat is greyer, and Garden Warbler is chubbier.

BLACKCAP   male 5½ in (14 cm) summer visitor

All upperparts, apart from the cap, are a greyish brown.

👁 Clear-cut black cap, grey face and breast.

★ Common summer visitor, scarcest in Scotland and Ireland. Requires trees or scrub. Female has reddish brown cap. Possible confusion with Marsh and Willow Tits, but note their whitish cheeks.

BLACKCAP female and juvenile 5½ in (14 cm)
summer visitor

All upperparts, apart from cap, are a greyish brown.
Cap is reddish brown.

👁 Clear-cut, reddish brown cap. Grey face and breast.

★ Common summer visitor, scarcest in Scotland and
Ireland. Requires trees or scrub. Male has black cap.
Female Whitethroat has obvious white throat, and Garden
Warbler is plain brown, no cap.

REDSTART male 5½ in (14 cm) summer visitor

Brown centre to reddish tail. Dark brown in wing.

👁 Reddish brown tail, frequently flicked. Obvious white
forehead.

★ Widespread, but local and not very common. Preferred
habitats are mature woods, or more open country with
good cover. A very distinctive bird, with no look-alikes.

REDSTART female 5½ in (14 cm) summer visitor

Whole bird brown or brownish, except for reddish tail
(with brown centre).

👁 Reddish tail. Rest of bird brown or brownish, with buffy
underparts.

★ Widespread, but local and not very common. Prefers
mature woods, or more open country with good cover.
Black Redstart is greyer; Garden Warbler and female
Blackcap have dark brown tails.

BLACK REDSTART female 5½ in (14 cm) summer visitor

Whole bird greyish brown, except for reddish tail with
brown centre.

👁 Reddish tail. Rest of bird greyish brown, including
underparts.

★ Rare breeding bird in the British Isles. A ground-loving
species, often nesting in old walls or on buildings. Blackish
male has white wing patch. Female Redstart has buffy
underparts.

ROBIN adult 5½ in (14 cm) resident

Plain brown upperparts and tail.

👁 Orange-red extends from breast, right up to the forehead.

★ Widespread and abundant in gardens and woodland
everywhere. A gardener's 'friend', but bold and aggressive
towards other birds. Male Stonechat and Redstart have
black faces.

ROBIN   juvenile 5½ in (14 cm) resident

Whole bird brown or brownish.

◉ Heavily 'scalloped' underparts. Brown overall. No wing, head or tail marks.

★ Widespread and abundant in gardens and woodland everywhere. Some other woodland juveniles show 'scalloping' (Redstart, Nightingale), but have red or reddish tails.

GARDEN WARBLER   5½ in (14 cm) summer visitor

Greyish brown overall, the underparts being paler.

◉ Plump. Lacks obvious markings, e.g. eye stripe, wing mark or bright colour.

★ Fairly common in England and Wales. Usually with trees, sometimes heaths. Tricky to identify – a fat Chiffchaff or Willow Warbler with no eye stripe! Perhaps a greyish-winged Whitethroat?

SPOTTED FLYCATCHER   5½ in (14 cm) summer visitor

Upperparts are a greyish brown. Crown and breast bear darker brown streaks.

◉ Flycatching behaviour. Streaked breast (not spotted!).

★ A widespread and reasonably common summer visitor, very visible due to prominent perching positions and flycatching behaviour. Inhabits open woodland and many larger gardens.

TREE SPARROW   5½ in (14 cm) resident

Chocolate-brown crown. Orange-brown on back, streaked. Plain rump and tail.

◉ Chocolate-brown crown, black cheek spot.

★ Increasingly local nowadays in its more traditional open country haunts, it is most likely to be mistaken for the grey-crowned male House Sparrow.

HOUSE SPARROW   male 5¾ in (14.5 cm) resident

Upperparts are rich brown from nape to tail. The back is heavily streaked.

◉ Grey crown, black bib.

★ Widespread and abundant, but prefers town areas and farm buildings. Female is rather nondescript, with clear pale eye stripe. Tree Sparrow is similar, but has black cheek spot, chocolate-brown crown.

HOUSE SPARROW female and juvenile 5¾ in (14.5 cm) resident

Back is mid-brown, streaked (with black). Paler, grey-brown underparts.

👁 Stout bill. Pale eye stripe. Lacks bright wing bars or underpart streaks.

★ Widespread and abundant. Prefers town areas and farm buildings. Male has grey crown, black bib. Beware confusion with the following females: Chaffinch, Greenfinch (wing bars); Redpoll, Linnet (streaked breasts).

WHEATEAR female 5¾ in (14.5 cm) summer visitor

Head to rump is a plain, soft brown. Wings darker. Dark brown 'T' on tail.

👁 Dark inverted 'T' on the white tail. Brown crown and back.

★ Reasonably common, and very visible in western and northern regions. Likes wide open spaces – cliff tops, moors and bare uplands. Male has grey back, Whinchat streaked back.

CHAFFINCH female and juvenile 5¾ in (14.5 cm) resident

Crown and back are greenish brown. Also brown hue to breast.

👁 Prominent white wing bars and tail feathers. Green-brown head, and green rump.

★ A truly abundant bird, found in flocks on farms, in gardens, hedgerows and woodland. Male has grey-blue crown. Winter Brambling has white rump, other finches lack double wing bars.

GREENFINCH female and juvenile 5¾ in (14.5 cm) resident

Head, back, rump and forewings are all a plain greenish brown.

👁 Prominent yellow wing and tail flashes. Greenish brown head and back.

★ Very common and widespread in gardens and woodland margins. Male has green back and yellow flashes. Beware confusion with female House Sparrow (no wing markings); juvenile Goldfinch (yellow wing bar).

BULLFINCH female and juvenile 5¾ in (14.5 cm) resident

Plain greyish brown back and forewings. The breast is a lighter shade.

👁 White rump, plain brown breast. (Juvenile lacks female's black cap.)

★ Common and widespread, they are found in woods and gardens. Noted as an orchard pest due to their liking for buds. The male has a bright pink breast. Young birds lack black cap.

DUNNOCK   6 in (15 cm) resident

Streaked dark brown back and forewings. Dark tail. Brownish flanks.

👁 Plain grey face and upper breast. Streaked brown upperparts.

★ Very common, very widespread. Known for skulking manner through scrub and bushy habitats. Thin bill and grey face distinguish it from sparrows and finches.

REED BUNTING   male 6 in (15 cm) resident

Warm brown back (heavily streaked), wings and tail. Hood can be brown.

👁 White moustache through black hood. (Hood browner in autumn and winter.)

★ Common and widespread, breeding near wet areas. At other times may be seen in fields or gardens. Often chooses to perch prominently. The female is much browner-headed.

REED BUNTING   female and immature 6 in (15 cm) resident

Warm brown head; streaked back, wings and tail. Brown streaks on breast.

👁 Heavy whitish moustache and white outer tail feathers.

★ Common and widespread, breeding near wet areas. Other times in fields or gardens. Male has black hood. Beware similarity to Skylark (shorter tail, head often shows crest) and Corn Bunting (plain tail).

MEADOW PIPIT   6 in (15 cm) resident

Upperparts medium brown. Dark streaks on back, breast and flanks.

👁 Like a small thrush, with white outer tail feathers. Weak 'tsip' call.

★ Common wherever found, liking open country and harsh conditions. Forms flocks in winter. Beware similarity to Tree Pipit ('teeze' call) and Skylark (bulkier, often with a visible crest).

TREE PIPIT   6 in (15 cm) summer visitor

Upperparts medium brown. Dark streaks on back, breast and flanks.

👁 Like a small thrush, with white outer tail feathers, and a 'teeze' call

★ Widespread, not particularly common, restricted to heaths and open areas with trees. Beware similarity to Meadow Pipit which calls 'tsip', and the crested, bulky Skylark. Neither perches in trees.

LITTLE RINGED PLOVER   6 in (15 cm) summer visitor

Back, wings, crown, rump and tail markings are all a plain, pale brown.

👁 Complete black breast band, and absence of any visible wing bar.

★ Uncommon summer visitor (and only to England), but very visible at gravel pits and other freshwater breeding sites. Slightly larger Ringed Plover shares breast bar, but has wing bar also.

ROCK PIPIT   6½ in (17 cm) resident

Upper parts dark grey-brown. Darker streaks on back, breast and flanks.

👁 Small coastline bird, with streaked breast, and grey outer tail feathers.

★ Readily visible in coastal habitat, feeding on insects. Numerically only fairly common. Meadow Pipit is the only real confusion species, but is paler with white outer tail feathers.

BEARDED TIT   male 6¼ in (17 cm) resident

Plain orange-brown back, rump, tail and flanks. Brown in wing.

👁 Black 'drooping moustaches'.

★ Very scarce. Restricted to reed bed breeding habitats, mainly coastal, and mainly in East Anglia. (Remote possibility of confusion with black, white and pink Long-tailed Tit.)

BEARDED TIT   female 6½ in (17 cm) resident

Plain orange-brown crown, back, rump, tail and flanks. Brown in wing.

👁 Brown above, with a long tail.

★ Very scarce. Restricted to reed bed breeding habitats, mainly coastal, mainly in East Anglia. (Remote possibility of confusion with black, white and pink Long-tailed Tit.)

YELLOWHAMMER   male 6½ in (17 cm) resident

Streaked back and plain tail are chestnut-brown. Partial breast bar.

👁 Almost all of head yellow (brighter markings than female), brown back.

★ Common and widespread in most open habitats with bushy cover. Repetitive song is often rendered 'a little bit of bread and no che-ese'! Female Reed Bunting has brown and white head.

YELLOWHAMMER   female 6½ in (17 cm) resident

Tail and streaked back are chestnut-brown. Streaked crown and underparts.

👁 Almost all of head yellow (darker markings than male), brown back.

★ Common and widespread in most open habitats with bushy cover. Repetitive song is often rendered 'a little bit of bread and no che-ese'! Female Reed Bunting has brown and white head.

SNOW BUNTING   winter male (both adults similar) 6½ in (17 cm) winter visitor

Nape, rump and breast marks are orange-brown. Darker crown, back and tail.

👁 Plumage is very variable, but large amount of white always distinctive.

★ A very rare breeding species, normally seen as a scarce winter visitor to eastern coasts and inland hills. Flocks form in winter, looking like 'a flurry of snowflakes'.

CROSSBILL   male 6½ in (17 cm) resident

Plain dark brown wings and tail. Back often shows a brownish hue.

👁 Crossed bills. Mostly red, but tints may vary from dull to a strong brick-red.

★ Quite uncommon (continental birds may swell numbers periodically), almost invariably in coniferous forest. A similar separate species exists in Scotland. The female is yellowish green.

CROSSBILL   female 6½ in (17 cm) resident

Plain dark brown wings and tail.

👁 Crossed bills. Mostly yellowish green. Young birds are greyer.

★ Quite uncommon (continental birds may swell numbers periodically), almost invariably in coniferous forest. A similar separate species exists in Scotland. Male red, but intensity varies.

NIGHTINGALE   6½ in (17 cm) summer visitor

All upperparts are a warm, rich brown. Tail notably reddish.

👁 Uniformly rich brown upperparts, when seen. Remarkable variety of song.

★ Not common, restricted to scrub and thin woodland in the south-east. Habitat or song (remarkable mix of staccato and fluty notes) exclude Whitethroat, Reed Warbler and Garden Warbler.

PIED WAGTAIL   juvenile 7 in (18 cm) resident

Crown and back are a grey-brown, with more brown on the breast.

◉ Long tail, repeatedly wagged. Brownish grey upperparts.

★ Very common and highly visible in virtually all habitats. 'Tizzik' call given from undulating flight. Adults have white faces.

SKYLARK   7 in (18 cm) resident

Upperparts quite a light brown, with darker streaking. Breast paler.

◉ Sustained trilling song given from high flight. Brown head is crested.

★ Very numerous, found in any open area. Obvious in song flight, but hard to locate on the ground. Meadow Pipit is slimmer, has no crest, 'tsip' call. Corn Bunting has brief jingling song.

CORN BUNTING   7 in (18 cm) resident

Upperparts quite a light brown, with dark streaks. Brown breast markings.

◉ Robust brown and white bird with a jingling song, and no white in tail.

★ Rather unusual these days, and local to grassland and cultivated habitats with perching positions. Yellowhammer shows yellow on head; Skylark gives sustained song from a great height.

DIPPER   7 in (18 cm) resident

Dark brown upperparts, belly and flanks. Chestnut at margin with white breast.

◉ Chocolate-brown and white markings.

★ Moderately common, restricted to fast-flowing streams in northern and western regions. Look for distinctive stocky bird patrolling a length of stream, or 'dipping' on a rock.

HAWFINCH   7 in (18 cm) resident

Plain rich brown back. Head, rump and tail lighter. Breast pinkish brown.

◉ Oversized bill, and white underwing markings (white, bordered black).

★ Widely spread, but distinctly scarce and secretive in its wooded habitat. Not as visible as Chaffinch with its obvious white outer tail feathers, or Bullfinch with white rump.

WAXWING   7 in (18 cm) winter visitor

Grey-brown upper back. Head and breast pale brown. Undertail, sienna-brown.

👁 Red 'wax' in inner wing, crest and yellow tail tip are all unmistakable.

★ A distinctly scarce visitor. Small groups turn up in variable numbers in unpredictable locations, almost always on berried bushes. Could just be mistaken for Starling in flight.

DUNLIN   summer 7½ in (19 cm) resident

Crown and back are a warm brown, with black 'scalloping'. Breast brownish.

👁 Black belly patch, downcurved bill.

★ Rather uncommon breeding bird, limited to northern moorland. Passage birds often retain black belly. In summer Golden and Grey Plovers are also black below, but have short, stubby bills.

RINGED PLOVER   adult 7½ in (19 cm) resident

Crown and back are a rather pale plain brown.

👁 Complete black breast band. White wing bar obvious in flight.

★ Breeds widely around coasts. Also a common winter sight on estuaries. Juvenile bird has partial breast band. Little Ringed Plover lacks wing bar. Dunlin is only similar in flight.

RINGED PLOVER   juvenile 7½ in (19 cm) resident

Crown and back a scaly, pale brown. Mask and breast band are similar or darker.

👁 Incomplete brown breast band. White wing bar obvious in flight.

★ Mostly seen on passage, around coasts and estuaries. Adult has complete black breast band. Much rarer Little Ringed Plover lacks wing bar. Longer-billed Dunlin only similar in flight.

COMMON SANDPIPER   7½ in (19 cm) summer visitor

Upperparts plain grey-brown, faintly streaked. Brown 'saddle' on neck.

👁 Brown 'saddle' mark around neck.

★ Quite a common wader, with a northern breeding range. Noticeable on passage with nervous bobbing, and low flight over water. Green Sandpiper is far darker, with an obvious white rump.

REDWING   8 in (20 cm) winter visitor

Plain brown on head, all upperparts and tail. Breast spotted with brown.

◉ Bold creamy eye stripe, brick-red flanks.

★ Numerous winter visitor, usually seen in flocks on open fields, or raiding berried bushes in gardens and hedges. Song Thrush, Mistle Thrush and winter Fieldfare all lack the eye stripe.

STARLING   adult 8½ in (22 cm) resident

Can appear all brown-black. Feather edges, wings and tail are truly brown.

◉ Glossy summer plumage (speckled in winter). Pointed wings seen in flight.

★ Abundant. Forms huge noisy flocks before roosting in cities or country cover. Juvenile birds are a plain 'mouse-brown'. Not likely to be confused with any other common bird.

STARLING   juvenile 8½ in (22 cm) resident

Plain 'mouse-brown' plumage all over.

◉ Plain 'mouse-brown' plumage all over. Pointed wings seen in flight.

★ Abundant. Forms huge noisy flocks before roosting in cities or country cover. Juveniles often seen begging from the darker adults. Not likely to be confused with any other common bird.

LITTLE OWL   8½ in (22 cm) resident

The back is brown, spotted with white. Underparts white, streaked with brown.

◉ Our smallest owl, 'earless', with pale eyes.

★ Reasonably common, widespread across England and parts of Wales, usually in agricultural or other open areas. Tawny Owls are considerably larger and inhabit more wooded country.

SONG THRUSH   9 in (23 cm) resident

Plain brown on head, upperparts and tail. Breast speckled with brown.

◉ Speckled breast, orange-brown upperparts and head.

★ Widespread and very common, the thrush of gardens and hedgerows. The Mistle Thrush prefers open fields, parks, and has greyish brown upperparts. Redwing has creamy eye stripe.

23

TURNSTONE   summer 9 in (23 cm) passage migrant

Rich, chestnut-brown markings on back and wings.

👁 'Tortoiseshell' back plumage, white on head.

★ Seen on passage around rocky coasts, usually very well-camouflaged. Summer dark-headed, dark-backed Purple Sandpiper should not confuse. Ringed Plover prefers sand and pebbles.

TURNSTONE   winter 9 in (23 cm) passage migrant and winter visitor

Grey-brown head, upper breast and markings on back and wings.

👁 Dark head and breast. White back and double wing bar distinctive in flight.

★ Does not breed in Britain, but is seen around rocky coasts, usually well-camouflaged. Some birds overwinter. Purple Sandpiper is very dark with a single wing bar visible in flight.

RUFF   female and winter male   9 in (23 cm) and 12 in (30 cm) respectively, passage migrant

Buff-brown breast, head and upperparts. Back 'scalloped' with brownish black.

👁 'Scalloped' brownish grey upperparts, and prominent divided white rump.

★ Small parties usually seen on passage on wetland habitat inland. Greenshank and Redshank show plain white rump and lower back in flight. Golden Plover in flight shows no white on rump.

RING OUZEL   female 9½ in (24 cm) summer visitor

Whole bird greyish brown, except for paler crescent on upper breast.

👁 Brownish white crescent on upper breast.

★ Quite uncommon, it appears rare due to inaccessible breeding grounds on high moors in north and west Britain. Female blackbird is obvious look-alike, with juvenile Starling worth a check.

BLACKBIRD   female and juvenile 10 in (25 cm) resident

Speckled brown breast, pale throat. Otherwise all a rich dark brown.

👁 Virtually all a rich dark brown. Even the breast is brown behind the speckling.

★ Often the most abundant bird in the region. Originally a woodland species, now familiar in any garden. Male is all black. Ring Ouzel has pale crescent; speckled thrushes are pale-breasted.

FIELDFARE   10 in (25 cm) winter visitor
Back and inner wing are a rich brown.

◕ Grey head and tail, brown back.

★ A numerous winter visitor to Britain, favouring open
country. It will raid gardens to strip berried bushes in hard
winters. Mistle Thrush is similar but is grey-brown above.

SNIPE   10½ in (27 om) resident

Breast, head and upperparts are brown or buff-brown.
Obvious back stripes.

◕ Flushes noisily, giving 'scaap' call in zig-zag flight.

★ Common and widespread, it is a bird of wet habitats in
open country. Often the first indication of the bird is the
explosive take-off. Woodcock is larger woodland bird.

LITTLE GREBE   summer 10½ in (27 cm) resident
Dark brown breast and upperparts. Chestnut cheeks and
throat. Dusky flanks.

◕ 'Sawn-off' fluffy tail. Chestnut cheeks and throat. Dives
when disturbed.

★ Widespread and reasonably common, but very wary.
Prefers quiet bodies of water, making it a difficult species
to observe. Tail distinguishes it from all usual waterfowl at
a glance.

LITTLE GREBE   winter 10½ in (27 cm) resident
Dark brown crown, nape and upperparts. Pale throat and
flanks.

◕ 'Sawn-off' fluffy tail. Buff cheeks and throat. Dives when
disturbed.

★ Widespread and reasonably common, but very wary.
Prefers quiet bodies of water, making it a difficult species
to observe. Tail distinguishes it from all usual waterfowl at
a glance.

MISTLE THRUSH   10½ in (27 cm) resident
Grey-brown upperparts and head. Breast speckled with
brown.

◕ Speckled breast, grey-brown upperparts and head.

★ Widespread. Very common on open parks and fields,
needing trees for summer breeding. Song Thrush has
orange-brown upperparts and orange 'wingpits'. Fieldfare
has grey head and tail.

NIGHTJAR   10½ in (27 cm) summer visitor

Whole bird is dark grey-brown, except for white wing and tail spots.

◉ After dark, long-winged silhouette and 'churring' call will distinguish.

★ Distinctly uncommon and very local to suitable heathland and wood-margin sites, mainly in the south. Kestrel-like silhouette may be seen at dusk, but 'churring' song is given all night.

TURTLE DOVE   10½ in (27 cm) summer visitor

'Scalloped' orange-brown outer back and inner wings. Plain upper back and rump.

◉ Neck patch. 'Scalloped' orange-brown outer back and inner wings.

★ Fairly common in the south and east, associated with trees and cultivated land. Song is a soft 'purring'. Collared Dove has a plain brown back and harsh song. Stock Dove has no white.

MERLIN   male 10½ in (27 cm) resident

Rust-brown streaked body and leading edge to underwings.

◉ Small bird of prey; pointed wings. Blue-grey above; faint moustache.

★ Uncommon. Favours upland, boggy and coast areas in north and west. Pursues prey with low-level dashing flight. Larger female is brown. Male Peregrine and Hobby have black heads and heavy moustaches.

WATER RAIL   11 in (28 cm) resident

Rich brown upperparts with darker streaks.

◉ 'Chicken-shaped' with long bill.

★ Uncommon, secretive and restricted to reed beds and marshy areas with cover. You could spend a lifetime just missing this bird! But a glimpse of its bill separates it from a Moorhen.

GOLDEN PLOVER   summer 11 in (28 cm) resident (the northern form is illustrated)

Golden-brown upperparts, including rump and tail.

◉ Varying amounts of black on belly; stubby bill; golden-brown upperparts.

★ Not very common, and easily missed on inaccessible, northerly upland moors. More visible on passage. Grey Plover is bulkier and silvery grey above. Ruff has white belly and divided white rump.

GOLDEN PLOVER winter 11 in (28 cm) resident

Golden-brown upperparts, including rump and tail.

👁 Golden-brown upperparts, including rump. Wing bar is barely discernible.

★ Not very common, but highly visible in winter flocks on lowland fields, mainly in the south. Grey Plover is bulkier, silvery grey above. Winter Ruff has white belly, divided white rump.

REDSHANK 11 in (28 cm) resident

Upperparts mainly greyish brown. Dark streaks on breast and flanks.

👁 Long red legs, obvious white 'triple triangle' flight markings above.

★ Common and widespread. Breeds on moors and marshy areas. Estuaries are best winter sites. Greenshank and Spotted Redshank lack wing markings. Black and white Oystercatcher, flight markings are similar.

RUFF summer male 12 in (30 cm) passage migrant

Variable. Most usual is dark brown ruff, buff-brown and black back.

👁 Extraordinary ruff and ear-tufts.

★ Rare British breeding bird, limited to a few wet meadows and marshy sites. Greenshank and Redshank have undivided white rumps and lower backs. At a distance Golden Plover shows brown rump.

PARTRIDGE 12 in (30 cm) resident

Upperparts a greyish brown. Chestnut-brown 'horseshoe' patch on belly.

👁 'Chicken-shaped', with orange-red face, grey neck and breast.

★ Quite common on agricultural land, often in small groups (coveys). Nervous, disturbs easily. Red-legged Partridge has white face and black 'necklace'; Pheasant is long-tailed.

COLLARED DOVE 12½ in (32 cm) resident

Upper back, forewings, rump and tail are all a plain, pale grey-brown.

👁 Black and white jagged collar mark.

★ Unknown in British Isles before 1952, this invader is now common and familiar in both gardens and farm buildings. Turtle Dove is very similar, but has 'scalloped' orange-brown back.

27

MERLIN female 12½ in (32 cm) resident

Dark brown upperparts. Underwings and body pale; body streaked with brown.

◉ Small for a bird of prey. Pointed wings, brown back, faint moustache.

★ Uncommon, restricted to upland, boggy and coastal areas in north and west. Low-level dashing pursuit of prey is very characteristic. Smaller male, Hobby and Peregrine are all grey-backed.

KESTREL male 13 in (33 cm) resident

Chestnut-brown back and inner wing (with black spots). Body buff to cinnamon.

◉ Hovers repeatedly. Grey head and spotted brown back.

★ Easily the most numerous bird of prey in the region. Widespread and very visible hovering over prey. Female has brown, barred upperparts. Merlin, Peregrine and Sparrowhawk do not hover.

CUCKOO juvenile 13 in (33 cm) summer visitor

Head and upperparts almost entirely a dark grey-brown (can be red-brown).

◉ The tail is long, brown, barred and wedge-shaped.

★ Widespread, fairly common, Cuckoos are easy to hear, hard to find. Their habitat varies with host parents' preferences. Female Sparrowhawk has banded tail, female Kestrel hovers.

MOORHEN 13 in (33 cm) resident

Back, wings and tail are all dark brown (not black).

◉ White flank stripes, red frontal shield over bill.

★ Common and widespread where there are freshwater sites with cover. Easily alarmed; undertail flashes warning. Coot has white frontal shield and plain flanks. Water Rail has long bill.

RED-LEGGED PARTRIDGE 13½ in (34 cm) resident

Upperparts are a plain, pale, grey-brown. Buff belly. Chestnut on tail.

◉ Chicken-like shape, black 'necklace'.

★ An introduced species, now locally common in south and east England on agricultural land. Partridge has an orange-red face. Female Pheasant is all brown with a long tail.

WOODCOCK 13½ in (34 cm) resident

Appears entirely rust-brown, although upperparts include buff and black.

👁 The only long-billed bird normally associated with woodland.

★ Widespread and not uncommon, but very difficult to spot on the ground. Usually seen as brown blur exploding from cover, or in circular display flight. Smaller Snipe prefers wet open areas.

BARN OWL 13½ in (34 cm) resident

Upperparts are beautifully patterned, buffy brown or even golden-brown.

👁 Palest owl, with white, heart-shaped face.

★ Widespread, but becoming uncommon due to loss of rough open habitat. Often nests in farm outbuildings. All other British owls are much browner.

LONG-EARED OWL 14 in (36 cm) resident

Grey-brown above. Underparts are buff with dark streaks. Reddish face.

👁 Long 'ears' erect when at rest.

★ Nocturnal. Widespread, but uncommon. Difficult to locate at roost in dense foliage, trees and thickets. Short-eared Owl inhabits open country; Tawny Owl is bulkier and 'earless'.

KESTREL female 14 in (36 cm) resident

Whole of upperparts are strongly-barred brown. Body buffy, streaked.

👁 Hovers repeatedly. Upper body barred.

★ Easily the most numerous bird of prey in the region. Widespread and very visible hovering over prey. Male has grey head and spotted back. Merlin, Peregrine and Sparrowhawk do not hover.

TEAL male 14 in (36 cm) resident

Dark head is mostly chestnut-brown. Speckled breast is buff coloured.

👁 Chestnut head with dark green patch. Green and black speculum white-edged.

★ Widespread, rather uncommon breeding species, fond of rushy pools. Winter migrants swell numbers dramatically, forming groups on almost any body of water. Female is brown, with same speculum as male.

TEAL   female 14 in (36 cm) resident

Predominantly brown, with most of the feathers on upperparts buff-edged.

◕ Brown. Small size obvious in flight. Green and black speculum white-edged.

★ Widespread, rather uncommon breeding species, fond of rushy pools. Winter migrants swell numbers dramatically; groups may form at any body of water. Other ducks are larger, note speculums.

RED GROUSE   14 in (36 cm) resident

Almost entirely a rich red-brown.

◕ Mostly red-brown with white-feathered legs. Male's red wattle prominent.

★ Normally associated with moorland and peat bogs, where they are common. Calls 'gobak-gobak-bak-bak'. Female Black Grouse is larger with longish, notched tail; Partridge is smaller farmland bird.

BLACK-HEADED GULL   summer 14½ in (37 cm) resident

Chocolate-brown 'hood'.

◕ Chocolate-brown 'hood' on head.

★ Common, the most visible inland gull. Breeds coastally, but also on inland marshy sites. Common and Arctic Terns are black-capped and have forked tails.

BLACK-HEADED GULL   immature 14½ in (37 cm) resident

Buff-brown in inner wing, visible when wing folded.

◕ Prominent white wedge in outer wing. Black band at tail tip.

★ Common, the most visible inland gull. Happily associates with man, seen at parks, fields and water sites. Immature Common and Herring Gulls have black tail tip, with all-dark outer wings.

RUDDY DUCK   male 15 in (38 cm) resident

Most of body is a ruddy brown.

◕ A small duck with an upright, stiff tail and a bright blue bill.

★ A North American species added to British list in 1971, when wild populations became established. Still scarce, but regular at some lakes and reservoirs. Female more grey-brown.

BAR-TAILED GODWIT   winter 15 in (38 cm)
passage migrant and winter visitor

Head, upper back, upperwings and breast are all a sandy
brown.

◉ Medium-large wader. Long bill (slight upturn). White rump,
no wing bars.

★ Uncommon, mainly seen on passage around coasts.
Black-tailed Godwit has longer bill and legs and prominent
white wing bars. Curlew and Whimbrel have long,
downcurved bills.

SPARROWHAWK   female 15 in (38 cm) resident

All upperparts are grey brown. White underparts barred
with dark brown.

◉ Brown bars on underparts, brown back. Round-tipped
wings.

★ Widespread, reasonably common with numbers
increasing. Rounded wings for woodland hunting with
dashing flight. Smaller male has grey back and brick-red
breast bars. Kestrel hovers.

PEREGRINE   juvenile 15–19 in (38–48 cm) resident

Upperparts are dark grey-brown. Buffy underparts have
dark brown streaking.

◉ Pointed wings, bold brown moustaches. Incredible
'stooping' dive on to prey.

★ Was endangered and is still unusual. Robust falcon,
adults with blue-grey backs. Outside breeding season it
favours most open habitats. Hobby and Merlin are more
agile and delicate; Kestrel hovers.

TAWNY OWL   15 in (38 cm) resident

Almost entirely brown. Reddish above, more buffy and
streaked below.

◉ The brown 'earless' owl of woodland. Gives hooting song
and 'kewick' call.

★ Easily the commonest owl in the region, but oddly
absent from Ireland. This is the woodland 'Brown Owl' of
'to-wit-to-woo' fame! Long-eared Owl is 'eared'; Little Owl
is tiny and prefers open land.

SHORT-EARED OWL   15 cm (38 cm) resident

Golden-brown and black upperparts, with dark carpal
patches mid-wing.

◉ Ground-loving, daytime-hunting owl of rough open country
(rarely farmland).

★ Quite scarce, restricted to rough and open country
away from interference. Highest densities in northern
England and Scotland, absent from Ireland. It is the only
owl likely in this habitat.

BLACK-TAILED GODWIT winter 15½ in (30 cm)
passage migrant and winter visitor

Pale grey-brown head, upperparts and breast.

👁 Large wader. Long bill (appears straight). White rump and wing bar.

★ Regular winter visitor, commonest in south at estuaries and inland water. Bar-tailed Godwit has shorter legs and no wing bar. Curlew and Whimbrel have downcurved bills, no wing bars.

COMMON GULL immature (1st winter) 16 in (41 cm)
resident

Brown speckles on head and neck, and brown on upperwings, but not on back.

👁 Grey back with brown, grey and black upperwings. Clear-cut black tail tip.

★ Common, inland and coastal. First-year Herring and Black-backed Gulls have less distinct tail bands, no grey in mid-upperwings. Immature Black-headed Gull has white wedges in outer wings.

STONE CURLEW 16 in (41 cm) summer visitor

Buffy brown head, upperparts and breast, all with dark brown streaks.

👁 Oversized yellow eyes, and prominent eye stripes and wing bars.

★ A rare visitor to the south, nesting on barren open ground. A 'thick-knee' rather than a curlew; no confusion is likely with any other species. 'Freezing' and stilted movements are characteristic.

WHIMBREL 16 in (41 cm) passage migrant

Dark greyish brown head, upperparts and breast. Dark brown crown stripes.

👁 Long downcurved bill and bold crown stripes.

★ Rather uncommon, frequently missed due to its similarity to Curlew, it prefers coastal fields and rocky shores. Curlew has extraordinarily long bill and finely marked crown.

BLACK GROUSE female 16 in (41 cm) resident

Almost entirely dark brown.

👁 Mostly dark brown with white-feathered legs. Long notched tail.

★ Uncommon, local to favoured sites, notably remote moorland and forest margins. Female Red Grouse is smaller, with stubby tail; female Capercaillie has orange throat, white on belly.

GUILLEMOT summer 16½ in (42 cm) resident

Head and upperparts plain, very dark brown (appears black in poor light).

◉ Seabird, with upperparts a dark matt brown. Pointed bill. Dark cheeks.,

★ Common maritime species, nesting on cliffs with suitable ledges. Black Guillemot shows prominent white wing patches. Razorbill has 'razor' bill. In winter, all are white-cheeked.

GUILLEMOT winter 16½ in (42 cm) resident

Crown and upperparts plain, very dark brown (appears black in poor light).

◉ Seabird with dark brown upperparts, dark pointed bill, white cheeks.

★ Common maritime species, widely seen around coasts, often storm-driven to harbours and inlets. Razorbill has 'razor' bill. Black Guillemot has white patch on wings. In summer, all have dark cheeks.

TUFTED DUCK female 17 in (43 cm) resident

Breast, head and upperparts dark brown, flanks slightly paler.

◉ Small crest. Bold white wing bars in flight. May show white at bill base.

★ Widespread and common. Breeds at large freshwater locations. After breeding, becomes highly visible, even on park ponds. Male has white flanks. Female Pochard is much greyer.

ARCTIC SKUA light phase 18 in (46 cm) passage migrant

Crown, most of wings, and upperparts to tail tip are dark brown.

◉ Dark brown and white seabird, pointed central tail feathers projecting.

★ Uncommon migrant, but the commonest skua in British Isles, some breeding on Scottish moor and cliff sites. Dark-bodied phase rarer. Confusion with immature gulls a remote possibility.

POCHARD female 18 in (46 cm) resident

Dark brown head, breast and tail. Greyish brown back, wings and flanks.

◉ Dark brown breast and greyish flanks. In flight, obscure grey wing bar.

★ Not very common breeding species, but widespread, mostly on lakes. Winter migrants swell numbers at reservoirs, lakes, etc. Compare with female Tufted Duck; brown back and flanks, white wing bars.

GOLDENEYE   female 18 in (46 cm) winter visitor

Plain brown head, clearly distinct from white on neck.

◐ Grey back, whole head plain brown. Nearly all of inner wing white.

★ Uncommon, sea and freshwater duck. Immature is duller, with no yellow bill tip. Male has green head, white face spot. Male Goosander and Merganser are a different shape. Male Wigeon has forehead blaze.

WIGEON   female 18 in (46 cm) mainly a winter visitor

Almost all of head and body are a reddish brown.

◐ Compact duck, reddish brown overall. Short, bluish, black-tipped bill.

★ A common winter visitor, flocking on large water bodies, the sea and coastal grasslands. Also passage migrant and scarce breeding species. Most plain ducks are darker-bellied (not Gadwall).

GREAT CRESTED GREBE   summer 19 in (48 cm) resident

Dark grey-brown crown, hindneck and back. Ear-tufts and flanks more orange.

◐ Dark crest and ear-tufts.

★ Much less common than might be expected, this species is highly visible and distinctive in summer on large bodies of open water. It is also widely seen at sea in winter.

GREAT CRESTED GREBE   winter 19 in (48 cm) resident

Dark grey-brown crown, hindneck and back.

◐ Long-necked water bird with a pink dagger-bill. Two wing bars in flight.

★ Not all that common, but highly visible on large bodies of inland water all year round. Also at sea in winter. Far smaller Little Grebe has a 'sawn-off' fluffy tail.

COMMON SCOTER   female 19 in (48 cm) winter visitor

Dark brown overall. Paler brown cheeks.

◐ Sea duck. Dark brown overall, except for paler cheeks.

★ Rare breeding species, but common enough around British coasts in winter. Forms into low-flying groups, only likely to be seen by sea-watching. Male is all black.

MARSH HARRIER   male 19 in (48 cm) variable status
Body and inner forewings are rusty brown. Crown and
leading edge to wings are sandy.

👁 Low, slow, hunting flight. Brown body with grey in wings.

★ A very scarce species, with migrants and the small
breeding population both being irregular in numbers.
Female Marsh Harrier virtually all brown. Hen Harrier has
white rump.

GADWALL   female 20 in (51 cm) resident and winter visitor
Most of plumage is either a rather pale greyish brown, or
buffy brown.

👁 Prominent white patch near sitting bird's tail. Orange on
side of bill.

★ Scarce breeding species, augmented by winter visitors.
Prefers slow-moving fresh water. Male is very grey overall.
Mallard, Pintail and Teal females all have white-edged dark
speculums.

SHOVELER   male 20 in (51 cm) resident and winter visitor
Bold chestnut flanks and belly.

👁 Remarkable spoon-like bill. Dark green head with white
breast.

★ Uncommon breeding species, augmented by winter
visitors. Prefers shallow water for dabbling, usually in
small numbers. Female is brown. Mallard and Merganser
males are brown-breasted.

SHOVELER   female 20 in (51 cm) resident and
winter visitor

Whole body and head is a warm brown. Wing tips are a
darker grey-brown.

👁 Remarkable spoon-like bill, brown body. Pale blue inner
wing in flight.

★ Uncommon breeding species, augmented by winter
visitors. Prefers shallow water for dabbling, often solitary.
Drake has dark head and white breast. Other similar ducks
have dark inner wings.

HEN HARRIER   female 20 in (51 cm) resident
Upperparts (except rump) dark brown. Tail banded. Paler
below, streaked.

👁 Low, slow, hunting flight. Brown bird of prey with a white
rump.

★ Uncommon, with a rather northern and western
breeding distribution. In winter visits fens, coasts and open
country. Smaller male is grey-backed. Marsh Harrier has a
brown rump.

LESSER BLACK-BACKED GULL   immature (1st winter)
21 in (53 cm) resident

Mostly brownish. Outer wing all dark, and dark band at tail tip.

👁 Brown back. Darkest outer wings of all the brown immature gulls. Black tail tip.

★ Fairly common, especially at breeding sites on coasts and inland. Immature Herring and Great Black-backed Gulls have grey panels in outer wings. Immature Common Gull has plain grey back.

BUZZARD   21 in (53 cm) resident

Variable amounts of brown in underwing. Upperparts consistently dark brown.

👁 Large soaring bird of prey. Underwing pattern consistent. Close tail bars.

★ Fairly common. Mainly westerly and northerly, requiring agricultural land with trees for breeding. Young Golden Eagle has similar shape and white in wings, but is a huge bird.

PHEASANT   female 21 in (53 cm) resident

Variable, from mid-brown to sandy brown overall; 'scalloped' back.

👁 All-brown bird with a long tail.

★ Originally introduced from Asia as a 'game' bird, now very common wherever there is woodland, but mostly seen on farmland. Male has red face wattle. Partridge is smaller and short-tailed.

PINTAIL   female 22 in (56 cm) winter visitor

Buff-brown overall, with 'scalloped' back. Brown speculum, dark wing tips.

👁 Short, pointed tail. Buffy colouring overall and obscure brown speculum.

★ Mainly rather uncommon winter visitor to coasts and estuaries. Also a scarce breeding species. Similar to Wigeon, but more ruddy. Mallard has blue speculum, Gadwall white, tiny Teal has green.

HERRING GULL   immature (1st winter) 22 in (56 cm) resident

Mostly brownish, including rump. Brownish tail tip, but not distinct.

👁 Brown back and rump. Grey panel in dark outer wings. Tail band indistinct.

★ Common round most coasts and inland. Other immature gulls: Great Black-backed has white rump, grey outer wing panel and is larger; Lesser Black-backed has white rump and dark outer wings; Common has grey back.

CURLEW   22 in (56 cm) resident

Most of head and body is a mix of light and dark brown. Dark wing tips.

👁 Very long downcurved bill. Brown head is finely marked, no bold stripes.

★ Common and widespread, except in south-east, breeding on rough, damp ground. In winter it moves to estuaries. Obvious look-alike is Whimbrel, which has shorter bill and bold crown stripes.

MARSH HARRIER   female 22 in (56 cm) variable status

Dark brown, except for creamy buff head and forewing markings.

👁 Low, slow hunting flight. Dark brown, with creamy buff head and forewings.

★ A very scarce species, with migrants and the small breeding population both being irregular in numbers. Male Marsh and Hen Harriers have grey in wings. Brown female Hen Harrier has white rump.

OSPREY   22 in (56 cm) summer visitor

Dark greyish brown upperparts, wing tips, mid-wing patches and breast bar.

👁 Bird of prey associated with water. Unbarred white belly and lower breast.

★ Once rare, but now a regular breeding species in Scottish forest areas. Diet entirely fish. Whitest Buzzards might confuse, but they have broader soaring wings and whole of breast is brown.

MALLARD   male 23 in (58 cm) resident

Rich brown breast. Dark brown in mid-back and outer wings.

👁 Blue (can be purplish) speculum. Tail curl. Green head and brown breast.

★ Commonest duck, widespread. Strains and intermediates can confuse, but speculum remains definitive. Male Shoveler has white breast. Male Red-breasted Merganser has white speculum.

MALLARD   female 23 in (58 cm) resident

Overall, plumage is a mix of darker and lighter browns.

👁 Blue (can be purplish) speculum with white margins. Whole body brown.

★ Commonest duck, widespread. Many female duck species are mainly brown, but most have white belly; no other has blue speculum. Beware similarity to Pintail, Gadwall, Shoveler and Teal.

EIDER   female 23 in (58 cm) resident

Uniformly dark brown, it can appear black out at sea.

◉ A uniformly dark, rather bulky sea duck, with a very triangular head.

★ Common. Breeds around all northern coasts, lining nest with breast down. In winter it is seen off all coasts. Common Scoter is more compact, with rounder head, and pale cheeks on female.

BRENT GOOSE   23 in (58 cm) winter visitor

Upperparts are dark grey-brown. Belly similar (or a whitish variant).

◉ Smallest and darkest goose, with whole of head black.

★ Large, highly visible winter flocks gather at southerly estuarine and coastal field locations. Otherwise sea-going. Barnacle and Canada Geese are dark-necked, but have white on faces.

SHELDUCK   adult 24 in (61 cm) resident

Bold chestnut chest band encircles the body. Chestnut on undertail.

◉ Build is mid-way between duck and goose. Broad chestnut band encircles body.

★ Common and widespread around coasts, usually nesting in rabbit burrows. Very visible at estuaries. Male distinguished from female and immature by the bulbous knob at the base of the red bill.

SHELDUCK   juvenile 24 in (61 cm) resident

Dark grey-brown crown, hindneck and upperparts. Imperfect chest band.

◉ Build is mid-way between duck and goose. Imperfect chest band. White cheeks.

★ Common and widespread around coasts, often at estuaries. Both parents have much bolder chest bands and dark cheeks, the male having a bulbous knob at the base of the red bill.

RED KITE   24 in (61 cm) resident

Reddish brown under forewings and on lower body. Upperparts darker brown.

◉ Large soaring bird of prey, with angled wings and forked tail.

★ Currently scarce, restricted to Welsh wooded valleys (attempts to introduce elsewhere). Juvenile has darker outer wing patches. Buzzard has quite different wing patterns and proportions.

CAPERCAILLIE female 24 in (61 cm) resident

Reddish brown crown and upperparts. Underparts barred with brown.

◉ Reddish brown upperparts. Orange face and throat. Long tail is stubby.

★ Scarce, and local to woodland areas in Scottish central highlands. Male is mostly black. Female Black Grouse is all dark, with a notched tail, and Red Grouse is all dark with a short, stubby tail.

PINTAIL male 26 in (66 cm) winter visitor

Chocolate-brown head. Brown shade in speculum.

◉ Long pointed tail. 'Finger' of white rising from breast into dark head.

★ Mainly rather uncommon winter visitor to coasts and estuaries. Also a scarce breeding species. Some similarity to darker-breasted, yellow-crowned Wigeon, but only at long distances.

GREAT BLACK-BACKED GULL immature (1st winter) 26 in (66 cm) resident

Mostly brownish, notably on back and much of upperwings. Brown on tail.

◉ Brown back, greyish in outer wings. Whitish rump, indistinct tail band.

★ Reasonably common, mostly on western coasts, more widely in winter. Other immature gulls: Lesser Black-backed has dark outer wings; Herring has brownish rump; Common has grey back.

BITTERN 30 in (76 cm) resident

Most of head and upperparts are a mixture of browns (with black).

◉ A large brown heron-type bird. Remarkable booming call is absolutely distinctive.

★ Very scarce breeding species, limited to a small number of reed bed locations, mainly in East Anglia. Rarely seen, except in low flight over reeds, but frequent calls will locate.

GREYLAG GOOSE 33 in (84 cm) resident

Most of plumage is a blend of brown and grey, brownest on back and wings.

◉ Large grey-brown goose, with a plain orange bill and pink legs.

★ Uncommon breeding species, but winter numbers swollen by migrants. Often seen at marshes and wet grassland. Brent, Barnacle and Canada Geese all have black necks and bills.

39

CAPERCAILLIE   male 34 in (86 cm) resident

Rich dark brown, from upper back to upper tail.

👁 Very large, robust bird. Dark plumage and long, rounded tail are distinctive.

★ Scarce, and local to woodland areas in Scottish central highlands. Female is mostly brown with orange face. Male Black Grouse has extraordinary lyre-shaped tail and white wing bars.

PHEASANT   male 35 in (89 cm) resident

Variable, usually with upperparts and body a beautiful golden-brown.

👁 Extremely long tail and red face wattle.

★ Originally introduced from Asia as a 'game' bird, now very common wherever there is woodland, but mostly seen on farmland. Female is all brown, but duller, also with a long tail.

GOLDEN EAGLE   35 in (89 cm) resident

Adult is a rich dark brown overall (immature has white in wings and tail).

👁 Great size is often sufficient to identify. Dark wings are long and narrow.

★ Scarce, mainly restricted to remote mountainous areas of Scotland. At a distance, size may not be obvious. Compare with Buzzard – check for shorter, broader wings and underwing markings.

CORMORANT   summer 36 in (91 cm) resident

Dark brown upperparts, wings and tail.

👁 Large dark seabird with a white face patch.

★ Fairly common and highly visible on most coasts. Nests on cliffs and small islands. Frequently seen at large bodies of inland water. Shag is wholly dark green and is sea-going all year round.

CORMORANT   juvenile 36 in (91 cm) resident

Dark brown upperparts, wings and tail. Paler head, throat, breast and flanks.

👁 Large dark brown seabird with a pale face patch and whitish belly.

★ Fairly common and highly visible on most coasts. Frequently seen at large bodies of inland water. Adult Cormorant and Shag are dark-bellied. Immature Shag has pale brown belly, pale chin.

GANNET juvenile 36 in (91 cm) resident

Youngsters mostly brown. Over three summers, the brown is replaced by white.

👁 Sea-going. Long, 6 ft (2 m) wingspan, narrow wings with varying brown speckling.

★ A successful species, breeding in only about 20 off-shore gannetries around the British Isles. Mostly seen well out to sea, sometimes in lines. Often dives from considerable height.

CANADA GOOSE 38 in (97 cm) resident

Brown back and wings. Underparts paler, with belly brownest.

👁 Goose with a white 'chinstrap' about face, and brown back.

★ An introduced species, now thriving in England, less common elsewhere. Breeds by water, from reservoirs to town ponds! Winters on grassland. Barnacle Goose is grey-backed, Brent is dark-headed.

MUTE SWAN juvenile 60 in (152 cm) resident

Whole bird is a 'dirty' grey-brown, unlike the pure white of the adult.

👁 Largest and heaviest bird of the region. Whole bird a 'dirty' white.

★ Widespread, reasonably common, and very, very visible. Normally in the company of parents, which are all white with red bills. Preference for slow-moving water.

COAL TIT 4½ in (11 cm) resident
White cheeks, nape and wing bars.

👁 Obvious white nape stripe.

★ They require trees, mostly conifers, where they are very common and widespread. Most alike are Willow and Marsh Tits, which have black napes and plain wings.

BLUE TIT 4½ in (11 cm) resident
White cheeks, forehead, eyebrow stripe and wing bar.

👁 Cobalt-blue crown.

★ Associated with almost any tree or bush, they are very common and very widespread. Beware confusion with Great Tit, which has black crown and black belly stripe.

CRESTED TIT 4½ in (11 cm) resident
Whitish face and underparts. White in crest.

👁 Obvious black and white crest.

★ In Britain they are located only in coniferous forests of northern Scotland, where they are locally common. Possible confusion with black-capped Coal Tit.

MARSH TIT 4½ in (11 cm) resident
Whitish cheeks and underparts.

👁 Glossy black cap, no wing bars or patches, and often-used 'pitchu' call.

★ Fairly common woodland species, restricted mainly to England and Wales. Willow Tit is very similar, but has a pale wing patch and gives 'eee' calls.

WILLOW TIT 4½ in (11 cm) resident
Whitish cheeks and underparts.

👁 Dull black cap, pale wing patch, main call a sequence of 'eee's.

★ Fairly uncommon woodland species, breeding mainly in England and Wales. Marsh Tit is very similar, but has unmarked wings and gives 'pitchu' call.

SISKIN   male 4¼ in (11 cm) resident and winter visitor

Pure white on belly and flanks, the flanks being heavily streaked.

👁 Streaked black, green and yellow bird, with a black forehead and chin.

★ Fairly common winter visitor, notably at garden peanut bags. Small breeding populations in coniferous woodlands, especially in Scotland. Female is plainer-faced. Beware similarity to unstreaked Greenfinch.

SISKIN   female 4¼ in (11 cm) resident and winter visitor

Underparts from throat to undertail are white or whitish, with streaking.

👁 Streaked black, green and yellow bird, with plain chin and striped crown.

★ Fairly common winter visitor, notably at peanut bags. Breeds in coniferous woodland locally, especially in Scotland. Male has black forehead and chin. Beware similarity to unstreaked Greenfinch.

GOLDFINCH   adult 4¾ in (12 cm) resident

White face band and spots under tail. Whitish underwing, throat and belly.

👁 Red, white and black head pattern.

★ Common and widespread (except in north Scotland), found on both open ground and in gardens. They love thistle seeds. Head pattern eliminates confusion with other species.

SAND MARTIN   4¾ in (12 cm) summer visitor

White underparts, except for breast bar.

👁 Swallow-type bird with brown breast bar.

★ Common and widespread, but declining. Requires banks or cliffs for nest burrow, usually in open country near water. May be confused with black and white House Martin, which has white rump and no breast bar.

REDPOLL   male (both adults similar) 5 in (13 in) resident

Breast, belly and undertail are white or whitish.

👁 Crimson forehead and black chin.

★ Reasonably common, but easy to miss. Often in large acrobatic flocks, they require trees, from heaths to conifer plantations. The adult male Linnet has a crimson forehead with a whitish chin.

TREECREEPER 5 in (13 cm) resident
White stripe over eye. White underparts.

◉ Tree-climbing behaviour (always upwards). Downcurved bill.

★ Associated exclusively with trees, mainly mature deciduous. Numerous and widespread, with no look-alikes. Actions and general appearance give rise to its description as 'mouse-like'.

WOOD WARBLER 5 in (13 cm) summer visitor
Pure white belly.

◉ Bright yellow throat and breast, and pure white belly.

★ Widespread, but quite scarce. Not easily seen in its mature woodland home. Far more colourful than either Willow Warbler or Chiffchaff. Also has an unmistakable trilling song.

SEDGE WARBLER 5 in (13 cm) summer visitor
Prominent whitish stripe over eye. Creamy white throat and breast.

◉ Very prominent whitish stripe over eye, with a black-streaked crown.

★ Common in reeds and other thick cover near water. Notable for loud churring song. Widespread across British Isles all summer. Compare Reed Warbler's plain plumage and faint eye stripe.

REED WARBLER 5 in (13 cm) summer visitor
Chin and throat white.

◉ Uniformly plain, reddish brown upperparts. A bird of reed beds.

★ Reasonably common in southern English reed beds. Female Whitethroat and chubby Garden Warbler are similar, but both prefer drier hedgerow and woodland habitat. Other similar warblers all show streaked plumage.

WHINCHAT 5 in (13 cm) summer visitor
White eye stripe, cheek borders and tail base edges. Male has white in wings.

◉ White eye stripe and border to cheek. Female duller than the male.

★ An open country species, locally common. Has favourite prominent perching places. Stonechat is quite similar, can occupy same habitat, but completely lacks the eye stripe.

STONECHAT   male 5 in (13 cm) resident
White wing patch and very prominent neck patch. Obscure
whitish rump.

◉ Entirely black head with prominent white neck patch.

★ Widely present, but with a markedly western
distribution. A bird of open country, frequently seen atop a
gorse bush. Female and juvenile are duller and more
streaked, as is Whinchat.

STONECHAT   female and juvenile 5 in (13 cm) resident
White wing patch.

◉ Streaked head and upperparts, small white wing patch.

★ Widely present, but markedly western distribution. A
bird of open country, often atop a gorse bush. Male has
prominent white neck patch. Whinchat has white edging at
base of tail.

PIED FLYCATCHER   male 5 in (13 cm) summer visitor
Pure white underparts and wing bar. Pure white outer tail
feathers.

◉ Black and white plumage only, with conspicuous white
wing bar.

★ Uncommon. Seen mainly on passage, or at favoured
woodland sites, usually deciduous (and mostly in Wales). A
hole-nesting species, it readily takes to nest boxes. No
look-alikes.

PIED FLYCATCHER   female 5 in (13 cm) summer visitor
White underparts and wing bar. White outer tail feathers.

◉ Brown and white plumage only, with clear white wing bar.

★ An uncommon visitor, exclusively associated with
woodland, usually deciduous (mostly in Wales). Compare
with Spotted Flycatcher (no wing bar), and female
Chaffinch (double wing bar).

HOUSE MARTIN   5 in (13 cm) summer visitor
Pure white underparts and rump. Note white-feathered
legs.

◉ Swallow-type bird with a white rump.

★ Common and widespread. Originally a bird of open
country. Now associated with man, building mud nests
under house eaves. Sand Martin is similar with obvious
brown breast bar, no white rump.

LITTLE STINT juvenile 5 in (13 cm) passage migrant

White underparts. Faint white wing bar. White rump divided by black.

👁 Tiny (smallest wader in the region), with a short, straight bill.

★ Rather uncommon, seen mainly on autumn passage, usually by inland water. Beware superficial resemblance to juvenile Dunlin (twice as bulky, longer downcurved bill).

LINNET male 5¼ in (13.5 cm) resident

Whitish chin. White patches on wings and tail are very visible in flight.

👁 Crimson forehead and breast, in summer. White on wings and tail, all seasons.

★ Widespread and numerous in most open country habitats. Forms twittering flocks outside the breeding season. Redpoll has black chin; Chaffinch has double white wing bars.

LINNET female and juvenile 5¼ in (13.5 cm) resident

White patches on wings and tail.

👁 White patches on wings and tail are very visible in flight.

★ Widespread and numerous in most open country habitats. Forms twittering flocks outside the breeding season. Redpoll lacks wing patches, and Chaffinch has double wing bars.

LONG-TAILED TIT 5½ in (14 cm) resident

Crown stripe, face, inner wing, outer tail and underparts are all whitish.

👁 Tiny bird with pink in plumage, and a disproportionately long tail.

★ Almost never on ground, they require trees or bushes, even if sparse. Numerous and widespread, forming small flocks outside breeding season. (Beware some similarity to ground-loving Pied Wagtail.)

LESSER WHITETHROAT 5½ in (14 cm) summer visitor

White outer tail feathers and throat. Whitish underparts.

👁 Dark grey mask, grey-brown back.

★ A scarce summer visitor, mostly found in south and east. Skulks in trees and scrub. Whitethroat has more reddish brown back, but beware faint mask on male. Garden Warbler is chubbier.

WHITETHROAT   male 5½ in (14 cm) summer visitor
White throat and outer tail feathers. Whitish underparts.

👁 Grey cap, white throat, and reddish brown back and wings.

★ A common summer visitor to scrubby locations. Female is brown-capped. Lesser Whitethroat is greyish above, with an obvious mask, and Garden Warbler is rather grey-throated.

WHITETHROAT   female and juvenile 5½ in (14 cm) summer visitor
White throat and outer tail feathers. Whitish underparts.

👁 Reddish brown cap, back and wings. White throat. Prefers dry scrubby habitat.

★ A common summer visitor to scrubby locations. Male is grey-capped. Reed Warbler prefers wet locations. Lesser Whitethroat is greyer, and Garden Warbler is chubbier.

REDSTART   male 5½ in (14 cm) summer visitor
Obvious white forehead. Pale belly

👁 Reddish brown tail, frequently flicked. Obvious white forehead.

★ Widespread, but local and not very common. Preferred habitats are mature woods, or more open country with good cover. A very distinctive bird, with no look-alikes.

BLACK REDSTART   male 5½ in (14 cm) summer visitor
Prominent whitish patch in wing.

👁 Very dark plumage, with frequently flicked, reddish brown tail.

★ A rare breeding bird to the British Isles, it is a ground-loving species. Often nests in cities in old walls or buildings. The drab female is browner and lacks the white wing patch.

SPOTTED FLYCATCHER   5½ in (14 cm) summer visitor
Generally whitish underparts.

👁 Flycatching behaviour. Streaked breast (not spotted!).

★ A widespread and reasonably common summer visitor, very visible due to prominent perching positions and flycatching behaviour. Inhabits open woodland and many larger gardens.

GREAT TIT 5½ in (14 cm) resident

Obvious white cheeks. Less noticeable wing bar and outer tail feathers.

◗ Black stripe from chin to belly (broader on male bird).

★ A very common bird, found wherever trees and hedgerows occur, and a familiar garden species. The smaller, blue-headed Blue Tit also has a belly stripe, but fainter and blue-grey.

TREE SPARROW 5½ in (14 cm) resident

Rather greyish white underparts and cheek.

◗ Chocolate-brown crown, black cheek spot.

★ Increasingly local nowadays in its more traditional open country haunts, it is most likely to be mistaken for the grey-crowned male House Sparrow.

WHEATEAR male 5¾ in (14.5 cm) summer visitor

Prominent white rump and tail markings. White eyebrow stripe.

◗ Black inverted 'T' on the white tail. Grey crown and back.

★ Reasonably common, and very visible in western and northern regions. Likes wide open spaces – cliff tops, moors, bare uplands. Female and Whinchat have brown heads and backs.

WHEATEAR female 5¾ in (14.5 cm) summer visitor

Prominent white rump and tail markings. Faint white eyebrow stripe.

◗ Dark inverted 'T' on the white tail. Brown crown and back.

★ Reasonably common, and very visible in western and northern regions. Likes wide open spaces – cliff tops, moors and bare uplands. Male has grey back, Whinchat streaked back.

CHAFFINCH male 5¾ in (14.5 cm) resident

Double white wing bars and outer tail feathers, very visible in flight.

◗ Prominent white wing bars and tail feathers. Grey-blue crown on male bird.

★ A truly abundant bird, found on farms in flocks, in gardens, hedgerows and woodland. Female is brown-headed. Winter Brambling has white rump; other finches lack double wing bars.

CHAFFINCH   female and juvenile 5¾ in (14.5 cm) resident

Double white wing bars and outer tail feathers, very visible in flight.

◉ Prominent white wing bars and tail feathers. Green-brown head, and green rump.

★ A truly abundant bird, found in flocks on farms, in gardens, hedgerows and woodland. Male has grey-blue crown. Winter Brambling has white rump; other finches lack double wing bars.

BULLFINCH   male 5¾ in (14.5 cm) resident

Brilliant white rump and undertail. Off-white wing bars

◉ White rump, bright pink breast.

★ Common and widespread, they are found in woods and gardens. Noted as an orchard pest due to their liking for buds. Female and juvenile are brown-breasted, the latter without the cap.

BULLFINCH   female and juvenile 5¾ in (14.5 cm) resident

Brilliant white rump and undertail. Off-white wing bars.

◉ White rump, plain brown breast. (Juvenile lacks female's black cap.)

★ Common and widespread, it is found in woods and gardens. Noted as an orchard pest due to its liking for buds. The male has a bright pink breast. Young birds lack black cap.

LESSER SPOTTED WOODPECKER   6 in (15 cm) resident

White-spotted wings, white-barred back. Also white on tail and head.

◉ White-barred back ('skeleton's bones'!). Male only has red crown.

★ Uncommon, restricted to southern Britain, and found in well-timbered habitats. Great Spotted Woodpecker is similar, but has obvious white 'shoulder-blades' and is nearly the size of a Blackbird.

BRAMBLING   winter 6 in (15 cm) winter visitor

White rump, belly and wing bars.

◉ White rump, orange breast.

★ Rather uncommon, fluctuating numbers arrive from September onwards. Beech woods are a favourite location, but they are seen in open fields also. Chaffinch is similar, but has a green rump.

REED BUNTING   male 6 in (15 cm) resident

White moustache, collar and outer tail feathers. Whitish underparts.

◉ White moustache through black hood. (Hood browner in autumn and winter.)

★ Common and widespread, breeding near wet areas. At other times may be seen in fields or gardens. Often chooses to perch prominently. The female is much browner-headed.

REED BUNTING   female and immature 6 in (15 cm) resident

Whitish moustache, throat, outer tail feathers and underparts.

◉ Heavy whitish moustache and white outer tail feathers.

★ Common and widespread, breeding near wet areas. Other times in fields or gardens. Male has black hood. Beware similarity to Skylark (shorter tail, head often shows crest) and Corn Bunting (plain tail).

MEADOW PIPIT   6 in (15 cm) resident

White outer tail feathers. Creamy white throat and underparts.

◉ Like a small thrush, with white outer tail feathers. Weak 'tsip' call.

★ Common wherever found, liking open country and harsh conditions. Forms flocks in winter. Beware similarity to Tree Pipit ('teeze' call) and Skylark (bulkier, often with a visible crest).

TREE PIPIT   6 in (15 cm) summer visitor

White outer tail feathers. Yellowish white throat and underparts.

◉ Like a small thrush, with white outer tail feathers, and a 'teeze' call

★ Widespread, not particularly common, restricted to heaths and open areas with trees. Beware similarity to Meadow Pipit which calls 'tsip', and the crested, bulky Skylark. Neither perches in trees.

LITTLE RINGED PLOVER   6 in (15 cm) summer visitor

White forehead, crown stripe, throat, collar, underparts and outer rump.

◉ Complete black breast band, and absence of any visible wing bar.

★ Uncommon summer visitor (and only to England), but very visible at gravel pits and other freshwater breeding sites. Slightly larger Ringed Plover shares breast bar, but has wing bar also.

BEARDED TIT   male 6½ in (17 cm) resident

White breast and some white in wing.

👁 Black 'drooping moustaches'.

★ Very scarce. Restricted to reed bed breeding habitats, mainly coastal, and mainly in East Anglia. (Remote possibility of confusion with black, white and pink Long-tailed Tit.)

BEARDED TIT   female 6½ in (17 cm) resident

Whitish throat, pale underparts and some white in wing.

👁 Brown above, with a long tail.

★ Very scarce. Restricted to reed bed breeding habitats, mainly coastal, mainly in East Anglia. (Remote possibility of confusion with black, white and pink Long-tailed Tit.)

YELLOW WAGTAIL   6½ in (17 cm) summer visitor

White outer tail feathers. Pale wing bars and eyebrow stripe.

👁 Repeated tail-wagging, combined with yellowish green back colouring.

★ Rather uncommon, preferring meadow and marshy breeding conditions, mostly restricted to England and Wales. Grey Wagtail is very yellow, but has grey face and extremely long tail.

YELLOWHAMMER   male 6½ in (17 cm) resident

White outer tail feathers.

👁 Almost all of head yellow (brighter markings than female), brown back.

★ Common and widespread in most open habitats with bushy cover. Repetitive song is often rendered 'a little bit of bread and no che-ese'! Female Reed Bunting has brown and white head.

YELLOWHAMMER   female 6½ in (17 cm) resident

White outer tail feathers.

👁 Almost all of head yellow (darker markings than male), brown back.

★ Common and widespread in most open habitats with bushy cover. Repetitive song is often rendered 'a little bit of bread and no che-ese'! Female Reed Bunting has brown and white head.

SNOW BUNTING   winter male (both adults similar)
6¾ in (17 cm) winter visitor

Large patches of white in wings, on tail, and also lower breast to belly.

👁 Plumage is very variable, but large amount of white always distinctive.

★ A very rare breeding species, normally seen as a scarce winter visitor to eastern coasts and inland hills. Flocks form in winter, looking like 'a flurry of snowflakes'.

PIED WAGTAIL   summer male 7 in (18 cm) resident

White face, underparts and outer tail feathers.

👁 Long tail, repeatedly wagged. Black and white plumage, with a black back.

★ Very common and highly visible in virtually all habitats. 'Tizzik' call given from an undulating flight. Summer females, and both sexes in winter, have grey backs.

PIED WAGTAIL   summer female and both sexes in winter
7 in (18 cm) resident

White face, underparts and outer tail feathers.

👁 Long tail, repeatedly wagged. Black and white plumage, dark grey back.

★ Very common, highly visible in almost all habitats. 'Tizzik' call from an undulating flight. Summer female has black bib which diminishes in winter. Summer male has black bib and back.

PIED WAGTAIL   juvenile 7 in (18 cm) resident

'Dirty' white face. White outer tail feathers and underparts below breast.

👁 Long tail, repeatedly wagged. Brownish grey upperparts.

★ Very common and highly visible in virtually all habitats. 'Tizzik' call given from undulating flight. Adults have white faces.

GREY WAGTAIL   summer male 7 in (18 cm) resident

White outer tail feathers, wing bar, and stripes above and below the eyes.

👁 Extreme length of tail, repeatedly wagged. Grey face, black throat.

★ Widespread, reasonably common. Almost always close to fast-running streams. Female and winter male white-throated. Yellow Wagtail has yellowish green back. Pied Wagtail, no yellow at all.

GREY WAGTAIL   summer female and both sexes in winter
7 in (18 cm) resident

White outer tail feathers and throat.

👁 Extreme length of tail, repeatedly wagged. Grey face,
white throat.

★ Widespread, reasonably common. Almost always close
to fast-running streams. Summer male has black throat.
Yellow Wagtail has yellowish green back. Pied Wagtail, no
yellow at all.

SKYLARK   7 in (18 cm) resident

White outer tail feathers, whitish underparts.

👁 Sustained trilling song given from high flight. Brown head
is crested.

★ Very numerous, found in any open area. Obvious in
song flight, but hard to locate on the ground. Meadow Pipit
is slimmer, has no crest, 'tsip' call. Corn Bunting has brief
jingling song.

CORN BUNTING   7 in (18 cm) resident

Pale throat and underparts.

👁 Robust brown and white bird with a jingling song, and no
white in tail.

★ Rather unusual these days, and local to grassland and
cultivated habitats with perching positions. Yellowhammer
shows yellow on head; Skylark gives sustained song from a
great height.

DIPPER   7 in (18 cm) resident

Pure white throat and upper breast.

👁 Chocolate-brown and white markings.

★ Moderately common, restricted to fast-flowing streams
in northern and western regions. Look for distinctive stocky
bird patrolling a length of stream, or 'dipping' on a rock.

HAWFINCH   7 in (18 cm) resident

White markings on wings (especially underwings) and tail
tip.

👁 Oversized bill, and white underwing markings (white,
bordered black).

★ Widely spread, but distinctly scarce and secretive in its
wooded habitat. Not as visible as Chaffinch with its obvious
white outer tail feathers, or Bullfinch with white rump.

SWALLOW 7½ in (19 cm) summer visitor

White spots in tail. Pale underparts.

◗ Red face. Long, forked tail.

★ Common and widespread in open country, often nests in farm buildings. Dark brown Swift has scythe-shaped wings; House Martin has white rump; Sand Martin has brown breast bar.

DUNLIN summer 7½ in (19 cm) resident

White underparts around belly patch. White wing bar and rump (divided).

◗ Black belly patch, downcurved bill.

★ Rather uncommon breeding bird, limited to northern moorland. Passage birds often retain black belly. In summer Golden and Grey Plovers are also black below, but have short, stubby bills.

DUNLIN winter 7½ in (19 cm) resident

Whitish underparts, white wing bar and rump (divided by grey).

◗ Grey-brown back. Longish, downcurved bill.

★ Commonest winter wader, found on many estuaries and coasts. Beware similarity to larger, stocky Knot, Sanderling with its scuttling runs, and the tiny Little Stint. Each has short straight bill.

RINGED PLOVER adult 7½ in (19 cm) resident

White forehead, collar, underparts, wing bar and (divided) rump in flight.

◗ Complete black breast band. White wing bar obvious in flight.

★ Breeds widely around coasts. Also a common winter sight on estuaries. Juvenile bird has partial breast band. Little Ringed Plover lacks wing bar. Dunlin is only similar in flight.

RINGED PLOVER juvenile 7½ in (19 cm) resident

Whitish forehead, collar, underparts, wing bar and (divided) rump in flight.

◗ Incomplete brown breast band. White wing bar obvious in flight.

★ Mostly seen on passage, around coasts and estuaries. Adult has complete black breast band. Much rarer Little Ringed Plover lacks wing bar. Longer-billed Dunlin only similar in flight.

COMMON SANDPIPER   7½ in (19 cm) summer visitor

White underparts. White wing bar obvious in flight.

◐ Brown 'saddle' mark around neck.

★ Quite a common wader, with a northern breeding range. Noticeable on passage with nervous bobbing, and low flight over water. Green Sandpiper is far darker, with an obvious white rump.

SANDERLING   winter 8 in (20 cm) passage migrant and winter visitor

Underparts and most of head white.

◐ Remarkable scuttling runs at edge of waves.

★ Not common, and almost exclusively seen on sandy coastlines in winter. Dunlin may cause confusion, but has a longer, slightly downcurved bill, and a 'stitching' feeding technique.

REDWING   8 in (20 cm) winter visitor

Whitish belly. Creamy eye stripe.

◐ Bold creamy eye stripe, brick-red flanks.

★ Numerous winter visitor, usually seen in flocks on open fields, or raiding berried bushes in gardens and hedges. Song Thrush, Mistle Thrush and winter Fieldfare all lack the eye stripe.

PURPLE SANDPIPER   winter 8½ in (22 cm) passage migrant and winter visitor

Whitish belly, undertail, divided rump and wing bar.

◐ A stout, dark bird of rocky coasts, with sooty head and dark back.

★ Rather uncommon, restricted to rocky coasts in winter, where it can be difficult to pick out. Much darker than Dunlin. Winter Turnstone has distinctive pied markings in flight.

LITTLE OWL   8½ in (22 cm) resident

White-spotted back. White eyebrows, throat, streaked underparts and legs.

◐ Our smallest owl, 'earless', with pale eyes.

★ Reasonably common, widespread across England and parts of Wales, usually in agricultural or other open areas. Tawny Owls are considerably larger and inhabit more wooded country.

SONG THRUSH   9 in (23 cm) resident

Pale, creamy underparts.

◗ Speckled breast, orange-brown upperparts and head.

★ Widespread and very common, the thrush of gardens and hedgerows. The Mistle Thrush prefers open fields, parks, and has greyish brown upperparts. Redwing has creamy eye stripe.

GREAT SPOTTED WOODPECKER   9 in (23 cm) resident

White 'shoulder-blades', wing-spots, face, throat, underparts and outer tail.

◗ White 'shoulder' patches.

★ Widespread, it is the commonest British woodpecker. Dependent on trees and hedgerows. Lesser Spotted Woodpecker is similar, but uncommon and only sparrow-sized.

GREEN SANDPIPER   9 in (23 cm) passage migrant

White belly, rump (seen in flight), eye stripe and finely spotted back.

◗ Dark back contrasts with white rump. (Appears black and white in flight.)

★ Uncommon migrant, seen at reservoirs, lakes and sewage farms. A few overwinter in southern England. Common Sandpiper has 'saddle' mark on neck. Redshank and Greenshank are larger and leggier.

TURNSTONE   summer 9 in (23 cm) passage migrant

Pure white belly. White on head, back and double wing bars.

◗ 'Tortoiseshell' back plumage, white on head.

★ Seen on passage around rocky coasts, usually very well-camouflaged. Summer dark-headed, dark-backed Purple Sandpiper should not confuse. Ringed Plover prefers sand and pebbles.

TURNSTONE   winter 9 in (23 cm) passage migrant and winter visitor

Pure white belly. White on back and double wing bars.

◗ Dark head and breast. White back and double wing bar distinctive in flight.

★ Does not breed in Britain, but is seen around rocky coasts, usually well-camouflaged. Some birds overwinter. Purple Sandpiper is very dark with a single wing bar visible in flight.

RUFF female and winter male 9 in (23 cm) and 12 in (30 cm) respectively, passage migrant

White belly and divided rump.

👁 'Scalloped' brownish grey upperparts, and prominent divided white rump.

★ Small parties usually seen on passage on wetland habitat inland. Greenshank and Redshank show plain white rump and lower back in flight. Golden Plover in flight shows no white on rump.

LITTLE TERN 9½ in (24 cm) summer visitor

Forehead, face below eye and all underparts are white or whitish.

👁 Forked tail, and yellow bill with a black tip.

★ An uncommon and vulnerable seabird, breeding locally on shingle and sandy coasts. Small size distinctive, but note much larger Sandwich Tern's bill is black with a yellow tip.

RING OUZEL male 9½ in (24 cm) summer visitor

Clean white crescent on upper breast.

👁 Clean white crescent on a black bird.

★ Quite uncommon, appears rare due to inaccessible breeding grounds on high moors in north and west Britain. Male Blackbird is similar (especially partial albinos, which often occurs in Blackbirds).

RING OUZEL female 9½ in (24 cm) summer visitor

Brownish white crescent on upper breast.

👁 Brownish white crescent on upper breast.

★ Quite uncommon, it appears rare due to inaccessible breeding grounds on high moors in north and west Britain. Female blackbird is obvious look-alike, with juvenile Starling worth a check.

FIELDFARE 10 in (25 cm) winter visitor

Whitish background to all underparts, and white underwing (seen in flight).

👁 Grey head and tail, brown back.

★ A numerous winter visitor to Britain, favouring open country. It will raid gardens to strip berried bushes in hard winters. Mistle Thrush is similar but is grey-brown above.

KNOT   winter 10 in (25 cm) passage migrant and winter visitor

Whitish underparts, eyebrow stripe and rather thin wing bar.

👁 A stocky wader, grey and white, with a straight bill.

★ Forms huge flocks at specific coastal and estuary locations. Dunlin is similar, with longish, downcurved bill. The whiter Sanderling scuttles with waves. Both are notably smaller.

SNIPE   10½ in (27 cm) resident

White belly. Pale head stripes.

👁 Flushes noisily, giving 'scaap' call in zig-zag flight.

★ Common and widespread, it is a bird of wet habitats in open country. Often the first indication of the bird is the explosive take-off. Woodcock is larger woodland bird.

LITTLE GREBE   winter 10½ in (27 cm) resident

Throat, cheek, flanks and all underparts pale. Fluffy tail whitish.

👁 'Sawn-off' fluffy tail. Buff cheeks and throat. Dives when disturbed.

★ Widespread and reasonably common, but very wary. Prefers quiet bodies of water, making it a difficult species to observe. Tail distinguishes it from all usual waterfowl at a glance.

MISTLE THRUSH   10½ in (27 cm) resident

Whitish underparts, white 'wingpits' and outer tail feathers.

👁 Speckled breast, grey-brown upperparts and head.

★ Widespread. Very common on open parks and fields, needing trees for summer breeding. Song Thrush has orange-brown upperparts and orange 'wingpits'. Fieldfare has grey head and tail.

NIGHTJAR   10½ in (27 cm) summer visitor

White spots near wing tips and at tail ends, visible if light permits!

👁 After dark, long-winged silhouette and 'churring' call will distinguish.

★ Distinctly uncommon and very local to suitable heathland and wood-margin sites, mainly in the south. Kestrel-like silhouette may be seen at dusk, but 'churring' song is given all night.

TURTLE DOVE 10½ in (27 cm) summer visitor

White tail margins, and undertail to belly. Black and white neck patch.

👁 Neck patch. 'Scalloped' orange-brown outer back and inner wings.

★ Fairly common in the south and east, associated with trees and cultivated land. Song is a soft 'purring'. Collared Dove has a plain brown back and harsh song. Stock Dove has no white.

WATER RAIL 11 in (28 cm) resident

White (and black) barring on flanks.

👁 'Chicken-shaped', with long bill.

★ Uncommon, secretive and restricted to reed beds and marshy areas with cover. You could spend a lifetime just missing this bird! But a glimpse of its bill separates it from a Moorhen.

GOLDEN PLOVER summer 11 in (28 cm) resident (the northern form is illustrated)

White around varying black belly markings. Faint wing bar.

👁 Varying amounts of black on belly; stubby bill; golden-brown upperparts.

★ Not very common, and easily missed on inaccessible, northerly upland moors. More visible on passage. Grey Plover is bulkier and silvery grey above. Ruff has white belly and divided white rump.

GOLDEN PLOVER winter 11 in (28 cm) resident

White belly, underwings and 'wingpits'. Faint wing bar.

👁 Golden-brown upperparts, including rump. Wing bar is barely discernible.

★ Not very common, but highly visible in winter flocks on lowland fields, mainly in the south. Grey Plover is bulkier, silvery grey above. Winter Ruff has white belly, divided white rump.

GREY PLOVER summer 11 in (28 cm) passage migrant

Whitish rump, wing bar and underwings. White around black underparts and face.

👁 Extensive black underparts, black 'wingpits', whitish rump.

★ Visible in this plumage around coasts in spring and autumn. A stout bird, may be confused with summer Golden Plover (golden-brown back and rump). Dunlin has brown back and longish, downcurved bill.

GREY PLOVER   winter 11 in (28 cm) winter visitor

Whitish rump and wing bar. Whitish below except for black 'wingpits'.

👁 Silvery grey upperparts with a white undivided rump. Black 'wingpits'.

★ On south and east coasts in winter. Stout, stubby-billed. Most confusion with slimmer Golden Plover (golden-brown back and rump), Knot and Dunlin (longer bills, white 'wingpits').

REDSHANK   11 in (28 cm) resident

Whitish underparts, and white 'triple triangle' flight markings above.

👁 Long red legs, obvious white 'triple triangle' flight markings above.

★ Common and widespread. Breeds on moors and marshy areas. Estuaries are best winter sites. Greenshank and Spotted Redshank lack wing markings. Black and white Oystercatcher, flight markings are similar.

SPARROWHAWK   male 11 in (28 cm) resident

White eyebrow stripe. Whitish barred underwings visible in flight.

👁 Barred brick-red underparts. Grey back.

★ Widespread, reasonably common with numbers increasing. Round-tipped wings for hunting in woodland with dashing flight. Larger female has brown breast bars and back. Kestrel hovers.

SPOTTED REDSHANK   summer 11 in (28 cm) passage migrant

White lower back and rump, barred tail (features best seen in flight).

👁 Body almost completely black.

★ Scarce, with summer plumage most visible on northerly migration in May. Seen on coasts, or marshy areas inland. Redshank and Greenshank are both much paler.

SPOTTED REDSHANK   winter 12 in (30 cm) passage migrant and winter visitor

White underparts, and on back.

👁 Long red legs, and white panel on back and rump (but not on wings).

★ Scarce, usually seen on coasts, or marshy areas inland. Confusion with brown-backed Redshank possible, but grey back will distinguish. Greenshank has greenish legs.

RUFF   summer male 12 in (30 cm) passage migrant

White belly and divided rump.

👁 Extraordinary ruff and ear-tufts.

★ Rare British breeding bird, limited to a few wet
meadows and marshy sites. Greenshank and Redshank
have undivided white rumps and lower backs. At a distance
Golden Plover shows brown rump.

GREENSHANK   12 in (30 cm) summer visitor and
passage migrant

White belly, rump and lower back. Throat and tail tip
flecked with grey.

👁 Long grey-green legs. Bill slightly upturned. White back 'V'
in flight.

★ Uncommon breeding species in northern Scotland only.
Mostly seen on passage at coasts, or inland water. More
grey than the brown-backed Redshank. Beware similarity
to red-legged winter Spotted Redshank.

LAPWING   12 in (30 cm) resident

White face, underparts, inner wing and rump.

👁 Crest, and flapping flight.

★ Common and widespread, a familiar bird of farmland
and open ground. 'Pee-wit' call gives the bird its country
name. At a distance, golden-brown Golden Plover might
appear similar.

PUFFIN   summer (12 in (30 cm) resident

White face and underparts.

👁 Multi-coloured triangular bill. At a distance, note whirring
wing action.

★ Fairly common, visiting off-shore islands to breed in
summer. Bill distinguishes it from larger relatives,
Razorbill and Guillemot. (Note that bill is smaller on winter
adult and juvenile.)

COLLARED DOVE   12½ in (32 cm) resident

White in jagged collar mark and also beneath tail tip.

👁 Black and white jagged collar mark.

★ Unknown in British Isles before 1952, this invader is
now common and familiar in both gardens and farm
buildings. Turtle Dove is very similar, but has 'scalloped'
orange-brown back.

MERLIN   female 12½ in (32 cm) resident

Pale eyebrow stripe, whitish throat. Whitish underparts and underwings.

◉ Small for a bird of prey. Pointed wings, brown back, faint moustache.

★ Uncommon, restricted to upland, boggy and coastal areas in north and west. Low-level dashing pursuit of prey is very characteristic. Smaller male, Hobby and Peregrine are all grey-backed.

HOBBY   13 in (33 cm) summer visitor

White chin, throat and side of neck.

◉ Small bird of prey with pointed wings, red leggings and distinct moustache.

★ Very uncommon, breeding on southern heaths and open country. 'Hawks' agilely on insects and small birds. Robust adult Peregrine is similar, but barred grey below. Male Merlin has faint moustaches.

KESTREL   male 13 in (33 cm) resident

Pale throat and underwings.

◉ Hovers repeatedly. Grey head and spotted brown back.

★ Easily the most numerous bird of prey in the region. Widespread and very visible hovering over prey. Female has brown, barred upperparts. Merlin, Peregrine and Sparrowhawk do not hover.

CUCKOO   adult 13 in (33 cm) summer visitor

Whitish background to grey-barred underparts. White spots on tail.

◉ The long, black, wedge-shaped tail has surprisingly obvious white spots.

★ Widespread, fairly common. Cuckoos are easy to hear, hard to find. They breed in many habitats, laying eggs in a variety of other species' nests. Male Sparrowhawk is brick-red below.

CUCKOO   juvenile 13 in (33 cm) summer visitor

Whitish background to brown-barred underparts. White nape spot.

◉ The tail is long, brown, barred and wedge-shaped.

★ Widespread, fairly common, Cuckoos are easy to hear, hard to find. Their habitat varies with host parents' preferences. Female Sparrowhawk has banded tail, female Kestrel hovers.

ROCK DOVE/FERAL PIGEON   13 in (33 cm) resident
All original Rock Dove-type pigeons have white rumps.

◉ Town pigeon-type. White rump. Black double wing bars and underwing borders.

★ Feral Pigeons (Chequers, black and white, Fantail and racing strains) are widespread and common. True Rock Dove now only on north and west coasts. Stock Dove has black upperwing borders, grey rump.

FANTAIL   domestic 13 in (33 cm)
All white.

◉ All white town pigeon-type, but with a fan tail.

★ A domesticated strain of wild Rock Doves, this is the familiar bird of the dovecote. It is the same species as Red and Blue Chequer, black and white town strains and racing pigeons.

MOORHEN   13 in (33 cm) resident
White flank stripes and undertail.

◉ White flank stripes, red frontal shield over bill.

★ Common and widespread where there are freshwater sites with cover. Easily alarmed; undertail flashes warning. Coot has white frontal shield and plain flanks. Water Rail has long bill.

COMMON TERN   13½ in (34 cm) summer visitor
Cheek, underparts and tail are white.

◉ Forked tail, black tip to red bill, black cap.

★ Only moderately common, but breeds by inland water as well as on coasts, so highly visible. Arctic Tern very alike, but whole bill is blood-red. Black-headed Gull has brown head!

BLACK GUILLEMOT   summer 13½ in (34 cm) resident
Pure white wing patch and underwing.

◉ Pure white wing patch, red feet.

★ Locally fairly common, mainly around north and west coasts. Guillemot and Razorbill are plain dark above, but beware similarity to Eider in late summer plumage, seen at a distance out at sea.

RED-LEGGED PARTRIDGE   13½ in (34 cm) resident

White cheek and chin.

👁 Chicken-like shape, black 'necklace'.

★ An introduced species, now locally common in south and east England on agricultural land. Partridge has an orange-red face. Female Pheasant is all brown with a long tail.

BARN OWL   13½ in (34 cm) resident

Palest owl, with whitish face and underparts.

👁 Palest owl, with white, heart-shaped face.

★ Widespread, but becoming uncommon due to loss of rough open habitat. Often nests in farm outbuildings. All other British owls are much browner.

LONG-EARED OWL   14 in (36 cm) resident

Very pale underwings (with dark mid-wing patches). Creamy 'V' above beak.

👁 Long 'ears' erect when at rest.

★ Nocturnal. Widespread, but uncommon. Difficult to locate at roost in dense foliage, trees and thickets. Short-eared Owl inhabit open country; Tawny Owl is bulkier and 'earless'.

KESTREL   female 14 in (36 cm) resident

Pale throat and underwings.

👁 Hovers repeatedly. Upper body barred.

★ Easily the most numerous bird of prey in the region. Widespread and very visible hovering over prey. Male has grey head and spotted back. Merlin, Peregrine and Sparrowhawk do not hover.

JAY   14 in (36 cm) resident

White rump, particularly obvious in flight. White in face, crest and wings.

👁 Brilliant blue wing patches.

★ Common and widespread where there are trees; absent from far north. Quite shy, but bright colouring and raucous calls make this the most spectacular member of the crow family.

MANX SHEARWATER   14 in (36 cm) summer visitor

White underparts and underwings.

◗ Black and white tube-nosed seabird. Tilting flight low over the water.

★ Surprisingly numerous, but hard to observe, as it breeds on off-shore islands which it visits at night. Visible during daylight, off coasts. Tube-nosed Fulmar is grey and white.

ARCTIC TERN   14½ in (37 cm) summer visitor

White cheeks, rump and tail. Underparts are greyish white.

◗ Forked tail, blood red bill, black cap.

★ Fairly common, but mainly restricted to northern coastal breeding sites. Common Tern is very similar, but red bill has black tip. Black headed Gull has brown head!

BLACK-HEADED GULL   summer 14½ in (37 cm) resident

White neck, underparts, rump and tail. Prominent white wedge in outer wing.

◗ Chocolate-brown 'hood' on head.

★ Common, the most visible inland gull. Breeds coastally, but also on inland marshy sites. Common and Arctic Terns are black-capped and have forked tails.

BLACK-HEADED GULL   winter 14½ in (37 cm) resident

White head, underparts, rump and tail. Prominent white wedge in outer wing.

◗ Prominent white wedge in outer wing. Reddish legs and bill. White tail.

★ Common, the most visible inland gull. Happily associates with man, seen at parks, fields and water sites. Common Gull has yellow legs and bill. Herring Gull has pink legs, yellow bill.

BLACK-HEADED GULL   immature 14½ in (37 cm) resident

White head, underparts, rump and tail base. Prominent wedge in outer wing.

◗ Prominent white wedge in outer wing. Black band at tail tip.

★ Common, the most visible inland gull. Happily associates with man, seen at parks, fields and water sites. Immature Common and Herring Gulls have black tail tip, with all-dark outer wings.

RUDDY DUCK   male 15 in (38 cm) resident

Prominent white cheeks and undertail. White belly visible in flight.

👁 A small duck with an upright, stiff tail and a bright blue bill.

★ A North American species added to British list in 1971, when wild populations became established. Still scarce, but regular at some lakes and reservoirs. Female more grey-brown.

BAR-TAILED GODWIT   winter 15 in (38 cm) passage migrant and winter visitor

Whitish eyebrow stripe and underparts. Prominent white rump and barred tail.

👁 Medium-large wader. Long bill (slight upturn). White rump, no wing bars.

★ Uncommon, mainly seen on passage around coasts. Black-tailed Godwit has longer bill and legs and prominent white wing bars. Curlew and Whimbrel have long, downcurved bills.

SPARROWHAWK   female 15 in (38 cm) resident

White eyebrow stripe. Whitish barred underparts and underwings.

👁 Brown bars on underparts, brown back. Round-tipped wings.

★ Widespread, reasonably common with numbers increasing. Rounded wings for woodland hunting with dashing flight. Smaller male has grey back and brick-red breast bars. Kestrel hovers.

PEREGRINE   male and female 15 in (38 cm) and 19 in (48 cm) respectively, resident

White cheeks and throat. Underparts and underwings whitish beneath markings.

👁 Pointed wings, bold black moustaches. Incredible 'stooping' dive on to prey.

★ Was endangered, still uncommon. Robust falcon, with female larger than male. Juvenile is brown. Breeds on cliffs, inland or coastal. Hobby and Merlin more agile and delicate. Kestrel hovers.

COOT   15 in (38 cm) resident

White frontal shield over bill.

👁 White frontal shield over bill.

★ Common and highly visible on most large bodies of fresh water. Gregarious in winter, sometimes in gatherings of hundreds. Moorhen has flank stripes and red frontal shield.

SHORT-EARED OWL   15 in (38 cm) resident

Creamy white underwings (dark mid-wing carpal patches and wing tips).

◉ Ground-loving, daytime-hunting owl of rough open country (rarely farmland).

★ Quite scarce, restricted to rough and open country away from interference. Highest densities in northern England and Scotland, absent from Ireland. It is the only owl likely in this habitat.

BLACK-TAILED GODWIT   winter 15½ in (39 cm) passage migrant and winter visitor

Whitish eyebrow, chin and belly. White rump and wing bar seen in flight.

◉ Large wader. Long bill (appears straight). White rump and wing bar.

★ Regular winter visitor, commonest in south at estuaries and inland water. Bar-tailed Godwit has shorter legs and no wing bar. Curlew and Whimbrel have downcurved bills, no wing bars.

KITTIWAKE   adult 16 in (41 cm) resident

Very clean white head, rump and tail, underparts and underwing.

◉ Yellow bill and black legs. 'Dipped-in-ink' wing tips seen in flight.

★ Perhaps surprisngly, the commonest British gull. Strictly maritime, it nests in colonies on cliffs, calling its name. Common Gull has yellow legs and white in wing tip.

KITTIWAKE   juvenile 16 in (41 cm) resident

Head, rump and upper tail, underparts and underwings all white.

◉ Black 'W'-mark on upperwings, black half-collar across neck. Black legs.

★ Perhaps surprisingly, the commonest British gull. Strictly maritime; may be overlooked for this reason. Calls its name at nesting colony. Immature Common Gull has brown in upperwing.

COMMON GULL   adult 16 in (41 cm) resident

Head, rump and tail, underparts and underwings all white.

◉ Pale grey back, yellow legs. Note white within black wing tips.

★ Not the commonest gull, but common inland and coastally. Northerly breeding on moors, lochs and fields. Herring Gull has pink legs, Kittiwake black legs, and winter Black-headed Gull red legs.

COMMON GULL   immature (1st winter) 16 in (41 cm) resident

White rump and underparts.

👁 Grey back with brown, grey and black upperwings. Clear-cut black tail tip.

★ Common, inland and coastal. First-year Herring and Black-backed Gulls have less distinct tail bands, no grey in mid-upperwings. Immature Black-headed Gull has white wedges in outer wings.

SANDWICH TERN   16 in (41 cm) summer visitor

White cheeks, neck, rump, tail and all underparts.

👁 Forked tail. Black bill with yellow tip. (Crested early in breeding season.)

★ The largest tern, rather uncommon, nesting in specific coastal colonies. Beware – crest lost in mid-summer. Other summer terns with white underparts have red or yellow bills and legs.

STONE CURLEW   16 in (41 cm) summer visitor

Pale eye stripe, face, throat and belly. Prominent, whitish, double wing bar.

👁 Oversized yellow eyes, and prominent eye stripes and wing bars.

★ A rare visitor to the south, nesting on barren open ground. A 'thick-knee' rather than a curlew; no confusion is likely with any other species. 'Freezing' and stilted movements are characteristic.

WOODPIGEON   16 in (41 cm) resident

White neck patches. Very prominent wing flashes visible in flight.

👁 Prominent white wing flashes visible in flight at considerable distances.

★ Abundant and widespread, usually near trees, although it feeds in open. Other pigeons and doves lack the white wing flashes, but Feral Pigeon and Stock Dove might confuse when seen at rest in fields.

WHIMBREL   16 in (41 cm) passage migrant

Whitish eye and crown stripes, rump, lower back, underwings and underparts.

👁 Long downcurved bill and bold crown stripes.

★ Rather uncommon, frequently missed due to its similarity to Curlew, it prefers coastal fields and rocky shores. Curlew has extraordinarily long bill and finely marked crown.

RAZORBILL   summer 16 in (41 cm) resident

White underparts, underwings and inner wing edges. White stripes on bill and before eye.

👁 Glossy black. Broad 'razor' bill with white vertical stripe. Black cheeks.

★ Fairly common maritime species. Nests on remote coastal cliffs and islands. Black and ordinary Guillemots are similar, but note unmarked, pointed bills. Winter birds are white-cheeked.

RAZORBILL   winter 16 in (41 cm) resident

White cheeks, underparts, underwings, bill stripe and inner wing edges.

👁 Broad black 'razor' bill with a white vertical stripe. White cheeks.

★ Fairly common but normally thoroughly maritime throughout winter months. Black and ordinary Guillemots are similar, but note unmarked, pointed bills. Summer birds are black-cheeked.

GUILLEMOT   summer 16½ in (42 cm) resident

White underparts, underwings and inner wing edges. (Occasional eye line.)

👁 Seabird, with upperparts a dark matt brown. Pointed bill. Dark cheeks.

★ Common maritime species, nesting on cliffs with suitable ledges. Black Guillemot shows prominent white wing patches. Razorbill has 'razor' bill. In winter, all are white-cheeked.

GUILLEMOT   winter 16½ in (42 cm) resident

White underparts, underwings and inner wing edges. White cheek, divided.

👁 Seabird with dark brown upperparts, dark pointed bill, white cheeks.

★ Common maritime species, widely seen around coasts, often storm-driven to harbours and inlets. Razorbill has 'razor' bill. Black Guillemot has white patch on wings. In summer, all have dark cheeks.

TUFTED DUCK   male 17 in (43 cm) resident

Brilliant white belly and flanks. Obvious white wing bars seen in flight.

👁 A crested duck, with brilliant white flanks (visible at great distances).

★ Widespread and common. Breeds at large freshwater locations. After breeding, becomes highly visible, even on park ponds. Female is brown-flanked. Male Goldeneye has cheek spot.

TUFTED DUCK female 17 in (43 cm) resident

White belly (sometimes also bill base). Obvious white wing bars seen in flight.

👁 Small crest. Bold white wing bars in flight. May show white at bill base.

★ Widespread and common. Breeds at large freshwater locations. After breeding, becomes highly visible, even on park ponds. Male has white flanks. Female Pochard is much greyer.

AVOCET 17 in (43 cm) resident and passage migrant

Mostly pure white plumage (except for crown, wing and back markings).

👁 Long, strongly upturned bill.

★ Having been extinct in the British Isles, it is now a very scarce breeding species, restricted to some shallow lagoon sites in East Anglia. It is also a scarce coastal migrant.

OYSTERCATCHER 17 in (43 cm) resident

White underparts and underwings. Bold white rump and wing markings.

👁 Pink legs, stout orange bill. Bold white rump and wing markings.

★ Quite common, breeds inland in north, otherwise on coasts. Noisy and highly visible. Noted ability to prise open shellfish. The mostly brown Redshank may confuse with similar markings in flight.

HEN HARRIER male 17 in (43 cm) resident

In flight, white rump very prominent. White underparts and underwings.

👁 Low, slow, hunting flight. Grey tail and upperwings with a white rump.

★ Uncommon, with a northern and western breeding distribution. In winter visits fens, coasts and open country. Larger female, and both sexes of Marsh Harrier, have brown backs.

MAGPIE 18 in (46 cm) resident

White underparts. White in outer wings, and on back.

👁 'Black' and white bird, with an extremely long, wedge-shaped tail.

★ Common and highly visible, but requires trees or at least bushes. Builds a remarkable football-shaped nest of twigs, very obvious in bare branches. Member of the crow family.

ROOK 18 in (46 cm) resident

Greyish white bare face and base of bill.

👁 Entirely black, with greyish white bare face and base of bill.

★ Common and gregarious, nesting high in tops of large trees in 'rookeries', usually near farmland. Carrion Crow has black-feathered face, Hooded Crow has grey body. Jackdaw has grey nape.

ARCTIC SKUA light phase 18 in (46 cm) passage migrant

Whitish face and belly. White patches in outer wings.

👁 Dark brown and white seabird, pointed central tail feathers projecting.

★ Uncommon migrant, but the commonest skua in British Isles, some breeding on Scottish moor and cliff sites. Dark-bodied phase rarer. Confusion with immature gulls a remote possibility.

GOLDENEYE male 18 in (46 cm) winter visitor

White underparts, inner wing, streaked outer back and unique face spot.

👁 Dark (green) head has white face spot.

★ Uncommon. Seen both at sea and on fresh water, making prolonged dives. Female has plain brown head and similar inner wing. Male Tufted Duck crested, with clear-cut white flank panel.

GOLDENEYE female 18 in (46 cm) winter visitor

White collar, belly and almost whole of inner wing.

👁 Grey back, whole head plain brown. Nearly all of inner wing white.

★ Uncommon, sea and freshwater duck. Immature is duller, with no yellow bill tip. Male has green head, white face spot. Male Goosander and Merganser are a different shape. Male Wigeon has forehead blaze.

WIGEON male 18 in (46 cm) mainly a winter visitor

White belly and inner forewing, both very prominent in flight.

👁 Yellowish blaze down the crown and forehead. White inner forewing.

★ A common winter visitor, flocking on large water bodies, the sea and coastal grasslands. Also a passage migrant and scarce breeding species. Female Goldeneye has a white collar.

WIGEON   female 18 in (46 cm) mainly a winter visitor

White belly. White margins both before and beside the speculum.

👁 Compact duck, reddish brown overall. Short, bluish, black-tipped bill.

★ A common winter visitor, flocking on large water bodies, the sea and coastal grasslands. Also passage migrant and scarce breeding species. Most plain ducks are darker-bellied (not Gadwall).

FULMAR   18½ in (47 cm) resident

White head, neck, underparts and underwings.

👁 Tube-nose (if seen). Bull neck; stiff wings in flight; quite unlike gulls.

★ A sea-going species, once scarce, now common around coasts. A cliff-nester. Clumsy on land, but a complete master of the air. Grey gulls and terns show black in wings, or on head.

GREAT CRESTED GREBE   summer 19 in (48 cm) resident

White face, throat and all underparts. Prominent inner wing bars in flight.

👁 Dark crest and ear-tufts.

★ Much less common than might be expected, this species is highly visible and distinctive in summer on large bodies of open water. It is also widely seen at sea in winter.

GREAT CRESTED GREBE   winter 19 in (48 cm) resident

White face, throat and all underparts. Prominent inner wing bars seen in flight.

👁 Long-necked water bird with a pink dagger-bill. Two wing bars in flight.

★ Not all that common, but highly visible on large bodies of inland water all year round. Also at sea in winter. Far smaller Little Grebe has a 'sawn-off' fluffy tail.

GADWALL   male 20 in (51 cm) resident and winter visitor

Prominent white in speculum, shows well on sitting bird. White belly.

👁 Greyest-looking duck, with prominent white patch near sitting bird's tail.

★ Scarce breeding species, augmented by winter visitors. Prefers slow-moving fresh water. Brown female shows orange on bill, prominent in good light. Male Wigeon has yellow blaze on head.

GADWALL   female 20 in (51 cm) resident and winter visitor

Prominent white in speculum, shows well on sitting bird. White belly.

👁 Prominent white patch near sitting bird's tail. Orange on side of bill.

★ Scarce breeding species, augmented by winter visitors. Prefers slow-moving fresh water. Male is very grey overall. Mallard, Pintail and Teal females all have white-edged dark speculums.

SHOVELER   male 20 in (51 cm) resident and winter visitor

White breast, outer back and tail. White wing bar prominent in flight.

👁 Remarkable spoon-like bill. Dark green head with white breast.

★ Uncommon breeding species, augmented by winter visitors. Prefers shallow water for dabbling, usually in small numbers. Female is brown. Mallard and Merganser males are brown-breasted.

HEN HARRIER   female 20 in (51 cm) resident

White rump.

👁 Low, slow, hunting flight. Brown bird of prey with a white rump.

★ Uncommon, with a rather northern and western breeding distribution. In winter visits fens, coasts and open country. Smaller male is grey-backed. Marsh Harrier has a brown rump.

BLACK GROUSE   male 21 in (53 cm) resident

White wing bar, wing spots, undertail and underwings.

👁 Robust black bird, with remarkable lyre-shaped tail and white wing bars.

★ Uncommon, restricted to favoured sites, notably remote moorland and forest margins. Males gather at courtship display areas called leks. Male Capercaillie has rounded tail.

LESSER BLACK-BACKED GULL   adult 21 in (53 cm) resident

White underparts, head, neck, rump and tail. Also spots in wing tips.

👁 Back and wings are dark grey (can vary in intensity); yellow legs.

★ Fairly common, breeds on level sites around coasts, but also inland. Pink-legged Herring Gull very similar to the palest Lessers. Much larger Great Black-backed also has pink legs.

73

LESSER BLACK-BACKED GULL   immature (1st winter)
21 in (53 cm) resident

White rump, whitish face and underparts.

◐ Brown back. Darkest outer wings of all the brown immature gulls. Black tail tip.

★ Fairly common, especially at breeding sites on coasts and inland. Immature Herring and Great Black-backed Gulls have grey panels in outer wings. Immature Common Gull has plain grey back.

BUZZARD   21 in (53 cm) resident

Variable amounts of white in underwing (but pattern is consistent). Individuals may be lighter or darker.

◐ Large soaring bird of prey. Underwing pattern consistent. Close tail bars.

★ Fairly common. Mainly westerly and northerly, requiring agricultural land with trees for breeding. Young Golden Eagle has similar shape and white in wings, but is a huge bird.

HERRING GULL   adult 22 in (56 cm) resident

White underparts, head, neck, rump and tail. Also spots in wing tips.

◐ Light grey back and wings, pink legs.

★ Common around most coasts, breeds on cliffs and dunes, venturing inland more in winter. Common Gull and the palest Lesser Black-backed have yellowish legs; Kittiwake has black legs.

HERRING GULL   immature (1st winter) 22 in (56 cm) resident

Pale face and underparts.

◐ Brown back and rump. Grey panel in dark outer wings. Tail band indistinct.

★ Common round most coasts and inland. Other immature gulls: Great Black-backed has white rump, grey outer wing panel and is larger; Lesser Black-backed has white rump and dark outer wings; Common has grey back.

CURLEW   22 in (56 cm) resident

White lower back, and barred rump. Whitish belly and underwings.

◐ Very long downcurved bill. Brown head is finely marked, no bold stripes.

★ Common and widespread, except in south-east, breeding on rough, damp ground. In winter it moves to estuaries. Obvious look-alike is Whimbrel, which has shorter bill and bold crown stripes.

OSPREY   22 in (56 cm) summer visitor

Most of head and most of underparts and underwings are white.

👁 Bird of prey associated with water. Unbarred white belly and lower breast.

★ Once rare, but now a regular breeding species in Scottish forest areas. Diet entirely fish. Whitest Buzzards might confuse, but they have broader soaring wings and whole of breast is brown.

MALLARD   male 23 in (58 cm) resident

White neck collar, speculum margins and tail feathers. Whitish underwings.

👁 Blue (can be purplish) speculum. Tail curl. Green head and brown breast.

★ Commonest duck, widespread. Strains and intermediates can confuse, but speculum remains definitive. Male Shoveler has white breast. Male Red-breasted Merganser has white speculum.

MALLARD   female 23 in (58 cm) resident

White speculum margins. Whitish underwings.

👁 Blue (can be purplish) speculum with white margins. Whole body brown.

★ Commonest duck, widespread. Many female duck species are mainly brown, but most have white belly; no other has blue speculum. Beware similarity to Pintail, Gadwall, Shoveler and Teal.

AYLESBURY   domestic 23 in (58 cm)

All of plumage white.

👁 All-white duck (except bill and legs).

★ One of several distinct domestic Mallard strains, often interbreeding with wild birds to produce mixed broods.

EIDER   male 23 in (58 cm) resident

Cheeks, neck, breast and back are white or whitish.

👁 Sea duck, mostly white above, mostly black below. Pastel green on nape.

★ Common. Breeds round all northern coasts, lining nest with breast down. In winter, seen off all coasts. Late in year it turns dark ('eclipse' plumage). Goosander and Shelduck have green heads.

RED-BREASTED MERGANSER   male 23 in (58 cm) resident

White collar and prominent inner wing. Whitish underparts.

◐ Green head shows double crest. White speculum and inner wing. 'Saw'-billed.

★ Rather uncommon. Breeds in north and west near water; includes sites far inland. Sea-going in winter. Male Goosander is white-bodied. Male Mallard has dark inner wing and blue speculum.

RED-BREASTED MERGANSER   female 23 in (58 cm) resident

White chin, white speculum. Pale throat and belly.

◐ Chestnut head has double crest. Pale throat. White speculum. 'Saw'-billed.

★ Rather uncommon. Breeds in north and west near water; includes sites far inland. Sea-going in winter. Female Goosander has smoother crest, and dark neck contrasts with pale breast.

BRENT GOOSE   23 in (58 cm) winter visitor

White patch on black neck. Tail and undertail pure white.

◐ Smallest and darkest goose, with whole of head black.

★ Large, highly visible winter flocks gather at southerly estuarine and coastal field locations. Otherwise sea-going. Barnacle and Canada Geese are dark-necked, but have white on faces.

SHELDUCK   adult 24 in (61 cm) resident

Most of body, inner forewing, tail and lower back are white.

◐ Build is mid-way between duck and goose. Broad chestnut band encircles body.

★ Common and widespread around coasts, usually nesting in rabbit burrows. Very visible at estuaries. Male distinguished from female and immature by the bulbous knob at the base of the red bill.

SHELDUCK   juvenile 24 in (61 cm) resident

White cheeks, throat and most of underparts.

◐ Build is mid-way between duck and goose. Imperfect chest band. White cheeks.

★ Common and widespread around coasts, often at estuaries. Both parents have much bolder chest bands and dark cheeks, the male having a bulbous knob at the base of the red bill.

RED KITE   24 in (61 cm) resident
Prominent white patches in outer wings.

◉ Large soaring bird of prey, with angled wings and forked tail.

★ Currently scarce, restricted to Welsh wooded valleys (attempts to introduce elsewhere). Juvenile has darker outer wing patches. Buzzard has quite different wing patterns and proportions.

MUSCOVY DUCK   domestic 24 in (61 cm)
White in wing. Very variable amounts of white areas on black body.

◉ Variable, the 'ugly' farmyard or village pond duck. A red knob on the bill.

★ Domesticated, a heavy-bodied duck mostly kept for the table. Originally from the Americas, not established in the wild in the British Isles. All Mallard strains are slimmer and possess tail curl.

BARNACLE GOOSE   25 in (64 cm) winter visitor
White face, tail base and most of underparts.

◉ Goose with white face and grey back.

★ Only common at favoured sites on north and west coastal grasslands, where they may gather in thousands. Canada Goose has white 'chinstrap'. Brent Goose has white neck patch. Both are brown-backed.

GOOSANDER   male 26 in (66 cm) resident
Almost whole of body whitish (cream and pink tinges). White inner wing.

◉ Whitish overall, including breast. All of head dark green. 'Saw'-billed.

★ Rather uncommon. Northerly breeding, normally by fresh water. More widely spread in winter. Merganser, Mallard and Shoveler males have dark breast or flanks. Male Goldeneye has face spot.

GOOSANDER   female 26 in (66 cm) resident
White chin and speculum. Whitish breast and underparts.

◉ Chestnut head, smooth crest obscure. Neck/breast contrast. 'Saw'-billed.

★ Rather uncommon. Northerly breeding, normally by fresh water. More widely spread in winter. Female Merganser is very similar, but note spiky double crest; pale throat lacks contrasts.

PINTAIL   male 26 in (66 cm) winter visitor

White belly and front of neck, with a white 'finger' rising into dark head.

👁 Long pointed tail. 'Finger' of white rising from breast into dark head.

★ Mainly rather uncommon winter visitor to coasts and estuaries. Also a scarce breeding species. Some similarity to darker-breasted, yellow-crowned Wigeon, but only at long distances.

GREAT BLACK-BACKED GULL   adult 26 in (66 cm) resident

Head, neck, rump and all underparts white. White spots in wing tips.

👁 Black back and wings, pink legs. Great size alone is often sufficient.

★ Reasonably common, breeds on cliffs, but oddly absent from eastern coasts (not Ireland). More widespread in winter. Lesser Black-backed is smaller, greyer-backed, and has yellow legs.

GREAT BLACK-BACKED GULL   immature (1st winter) 26 in (66 cm) resident

Whitish head, neck, rump and underparts.

👁 Brown back, greyish in outer wings. Whitish rump, indistinct tail band.

★ Reasonably common, mostly on western coasts, more widely in winter. Other immature gulls: Lesser Black-backed has dark outer wings; Herring has brownish rump; Common has grey back.

GREY HERON   35 in (89 cm) resident

Greyish white head, neck and underparts.

👁 Extremely long neck (folded back in flight). Grey back.

★ Not numerically common at all, but a big bird, often out in the open and highly visible. Builds platform nests in tree tops, often in colonies (can get very noisy!). Bittern similar, but very brown.

CORMORANT   summer 36 in (91 cm) resident

White face patch, and (summer only) white thigh patch.

👁 Large dark seabird with a white face patch.

★ Fairly common and highly visible on most coasts. Nests on cliffs and small islands. Frequently seen at large bodies of inland water. Shag is wholly dark green and is sea-going all year round.

CORMORANT   juvenile 36 in (91 cm) resident

Pale face patch, whitish belly.

👁 Large dark brown seabird with a pale face patch and whitish belly.

★ Fairly common, and highly visible on most coasts. Frequently seen at large bodies of inland water. Adult Cormorant and Shag are dark-bellied. Immature Shag has pale brown belly, pale chin.

GANNET   adult 36 in (91 cm) resident

Whole body, except head, is white. White inner wings also.

👁 Sea-going. Long, 6 ft (2 m) wingspan, white wings, black-tipped. Dramatic diver.

★ A successful species, breeding in only about 20 off-shore gannetries around the British Isles. Mostly seen well out to sea, sometimes in lines. Adult plumage from fourth year.

GANNET   juvenile 36 in (91 cm) resident

Youngest birds speckled only. For 3 summers, body and wings get whiter.

👁 Sea-going. Long, 6 ft (2 m) wingspan, narrow wings with varying brown speckling.

★ A successful species, breeding in only about 20 off-shore gannetries around the British Isles. Mostly seen well out to sea, sometimes in lines. Often dives from considerable height.

CANADA GOOSE   38 in (97 cm) resident

White uppertail, undertail and 'chinstrap' on face. Whitish breast.

👁 Goose with a white 'chinstrap' about face and brown back.

★ An introduced species, now thriving in England, less common elsewhere. Breeds by water, from reservoirs to town ponds! Winters on grassland. Barnacle Goose is grey-backed, Brent is dark-headed.

BEWICK'S SWAN   48 in (122 cm) winter visitor

All plumage is white.

👁 Shortest-necked, stocky swan. Bill half yellow (rather rounded border).

★ A scarce winter visitor, usually forming flocks at favoured water and grassland locations. Whooper Swan has a more extensive 'triangle' of yellow down bill. Mute Swan has a red bill.

WHOOPER SWAN   58 in (147 cm) winter visitor

All plumage is white.

◉ Extensive 'triangle' of yellow down bill. A large, long-necked swan.

★ Quite uncommon, forming winter flocks at favoured water and grassland locations. Bewick's Swan's bill is half yellow, the border being rather rounded. Mute Swan has a red bill.

MUTE SWAN   adult 60 in (152 cm) resident

All plumage is white.

◉ Largest and heaviest bird of the region. Swan with a red bill.

★ Widespread, reasonably common, very, very visible. Builds a huge nest near slow-moving water. Male has large black knob at bill base. Whooper and Bewick's Swans have yellow in bills.

MUTE SWAN   juvenile 60 in (152 cm) resident

The whole bird is a 'dirty' white, quite grey-brown at some ages.

◉ Largest and heaviest bird of the region. Whole bird a 'dirty' white.

★ Widespread, reasonably common, and very, very visible. Normally in the company of parents, which are all white with red bills. Preference for slow-moving water.

COAL TIT 4½ in (11 cm) resident

Upperparts grey from neck to tail tip.

👁 Obvious white nape stripe.

★ They require trees, mostly conifers, where they are very common and widespread. Most alike are Willow and Marsh Tits, which have black napes and plain wings.

DARTFORD WARBLER 5 in (13 cm) resident

Male has a very dark grey head, and greyish tones in the back and tail.

👁 Underparts are a dark wine-red. Long tail is often cocked.

★ Very uncommon, only a few hundred birds being found in gorse-covered areas of southern England. Really a Mediterranean species, this is the very northern tip of its range.

LESSER WHITETHROAT 5½ in (14 cm) summer visitor

Pale grey head, dark grey mask (notably in the male). Back and tail grey-brown.

👁 Dark grey mask, grey-brown back

★ A scarce summer visitor, mostly found in south and east. Skulks in trees and scrub. Whitethroat has more reddish brown back, but beware faint mask on male. Garden Warbler is chubbier.

WHITETHROAT male 5½ in (14 cm) summer visitor

Medium grey head, (beware – sometimes with a hint of a darker mask!).

👁 Grey cap, white throat, and reddish brown back and wings.

★ A common summer visitor to scrubby locations. Female is brown-capped. Lesser Whitethroat is greyish above, with an obvious mask, and Garden Warbler is rather grey-throated.

BLACKCAP male 5½ in (14 cm) summer visitor

Grey face, throat and breast. Upperparts and tail greyish brown.

👁 Clear-cut black cap, grey face and breast.

★ Common summer visitor, scarcest in Scotland and Ireland. Requires trees or scrub. Female has reddish brown cap. Possible confusion with Marsh and Willow Tits, but note their whitish cheeks.

BLACKCAP   female and juvenile 5½ in (14 cm)
summer visitor

Grey face. Throat and breast are light grey-brown,
upperparts much darker.

👁 Clear-cut reddish brown cap. Grey face and breast.

★ Common summer visitor, scarcest in Scotland and
Ireland. Requires trees or scrub. Male has black cap.
Female Whitethroat has obvious white throat, and Garden
Warbler is plain brown, no cap.

REDSTART   male 5½ in (14 cm) summer visitor

Pale grey crown, nape and back. Grey in wings also.

👁 Reddish brown tail, frequently flicked. Obvious white
forehead.

★ Widespread, but local and not very common. Preferred
habitats are mature woods, or more open country with
good cover. A very distinctive bird, with no look-alikes.

NUTHATCH   5½ in (14 cm) resident

Notably bluish grey upperparts.

👁 Climbs about tree trunks in any direction. Blue-grey
upperparts.

★ Reasonably common throughout Wales and southern
England, invariably associated with trunks of trees.
Treecreeper shares habitat, but is mainly brown and only
ascends trunks.

HOUSE SPARROW   male 5¾ in (14.5 cm) resident

Grey crown and rump.

👁 Grey crown, black bib.

★ Widespread and abundant, but prefers town areas and
farm buildings. Female is rather nondescript, with clear
pale eye stripe. Tree Sparrow is similar, but has black
cheek spot, chocolate-brown crown.

WHEATEAR   male 5¾ in (14.5 cm) summer visitor

A clean, pale grey crown and back.

👁 Black inverted 'T' on the white tail. Grey crown and back.

★ Reasonably common, and very visible in western and
northern regions. Likes wide open spaces – cliff tops,
moors, bare uplands. Female and Whinchat have brown
heads and backs.

BULLFINCH   male 5¾ in (14.5 cm) resident

Plain grey nape, back and forewings.

◐ White rump, bright pink breast.

★ Common and widespread, it is found in woods and gardens. Noted as an orchard pest due to its liking for buds. Female and juvenile are brown-breasted, the latter without the cap.

DUNNOCK   6 in (15 cm) resident

Grey about face, on throat, breast and most of underparts.

◐ Plain grey face and upper breast. Streaked brown upperparts.

★ Very common, very widespread. Known for skulking manner through scrub and bushy habitats. Thin bill and grey face distinguish it from sparrows and finches

BRAMBLING   winter 6 in (15 cm) winter visitor

Variable amounts of grey on head and upper back.

◐ White rump, orange breast.

★ Rather uncommon, fluctuating numbers arrive from September onwards. Beech woods are a favourite location, but they are seen in open fields also. Chaffinch is similar, but has a green rump.

ROCK PIPIT   6½ in (17 cm) resident

Head to tail, all upperparts are greyish brown. Grey outer tail feathers.

◐ Small coastline bird, with streaked breast, and grey outer tail feathers.

★ Readily visible in coastal habitat, feeding on insects. Numerically only fairly common. Meadow Pipit is the only real confusion species, but is paler with white outer tail feathers.

BEARDED TIT   male 6½ in (17 cm) resident

Most of head is a delicate bluish grey.

◐ Black 'drooping moustaches'.

★ Very scarce. Restricted to reed bed breeding habitats, mainly coastal, and mainly in East Anglia. (Remote possibility of confusion with black, white and pink Long-tailed Tit.)

NIGHTINGALE   6½ in (17 cm) summer visitor

Underparts are a pale greyish brown.

👁 Uniformly rich brown upperparts, when seen. Remarkable variety of song.

★ Not common, restricted to scrub and thin woodland in the south-east. Habitat or song (remarkable mix of staccato and fluty notes) exclude Whitethroat, Reed Warbler and Garden Warbler.

PIED WAGTAIL   summer female and both sexes winter 7 in (18 cm) resident

Back distinctly grey (unlike black back of male). Some grey on flanks.

👁 Long tail, repeatedly wagged. Black and white plumage, dark grey back.

★ Very common, highly visible in almost all habitats. 'Tizzik' call from an undulating flight. Summer female has black bib which diminishes in winter. Summer male has black bib and back.

PIED WAGTAIL   juvenile 7 in (18 cm) resident

Crown and back are a 'dirty' brownish grey.

👁 Long tail, repeatedly wagged. Brownish grey upperparts.

★ Very common and highly visible in virtually all habitats. 'Tizzik' call given from undulating flight. Adults have white faces.

GREY WAGTAIL   summer male 7 in (18 cm) resident

Plain blue-grey face, crown, back and forewings.

👁 Extreme length of tail, repeatedly wagged. Grey face, black throat.

★ Widespread, reasonably common. Almost always close to fast-running streams. Female and winter male white-throated. Yellow Wagtail has yellowish green back. Pied Wagtail, no yellow at all.

GREY WAGTAIL   summer female and both sexes in winter 7 in (18 cm) resident

Plain blue-grey face, crown, back and forewings.

👁 Extreme length of tail, repeatedly wagged. Grey face, white throat.

★ Widespread, reasonably common. Almost always close to fast-running streams. Summer male has black throat. Yellow Wagtail has yellowish green back. Pied Wagtail, no yellow at all.

DUNLIN   winter 7½ in (19 cm) resident

All upperparts in grey tones, with grey streaking on breast.

◐ Grey-brown back. Longish, downcurved bill.

★ Commonest winter wader, found on many estuaries and coasts. Beware similarity to larger, stocky Knot, Sanderling with its scuttling runs, and the tiny Little Stint. Each has short straight bill.

SANDERLING   winter 8 in (20 cm) passage migrant and winter visitor

Very pale grey face and upperparts.

◐ Remarkable scuttling runs at edge of waves.

★ Not common, and almost exclusively seen on sandy coastlines in winter. Dunlin may cause confusion, but has a longer, slightly downcurved bill, and a 'stitching' feeding technique.

PURPLE SANDPIPER   winter 8½ in (22 cm) passage migrant and winter visitor

Very dark slate-grey head, upperparts and breast. Flanks streaked.

◐ A stout, dark bird of rocky coasts, with sooty head and dark back.

★ Rather uncommon, restricted to rocky coasts in winter, where it can be difficult to pick out. Much darker than Dunlin. Winter Turnstone has distinctive pied markings in flight.

LITTLE TERN   9½ in (24 cm) summer visitor

Plain pale grey upperparts and upperwings.

◐ Forked tail, and yellow bill with a black tip.

★ An uncommon and vulnerable seabird, breeding locally on shingle and sandy coasts. Small size distinctive, but note much larger Sandwich Tern's bill is black with a yellow tip.

BLACK TERN   summer 9½ in (24 cm) passage migrant

Plain grey wings and upperparts from neck to tail.

◐ Forked tail and black body.

★ Rather uncommon, usually seen in small groups on passage at lakes, reservoirs, etc. Buoyant flight and black body identify in spring (but beware autumn juveniles – white-bodied!).

FIELDFARE   10 in (25 cm) winter visitor

Plain grey head and rump. Some grey tones in flank markings.

◉ Grey head and tail, brown back.

★ A numerous winter visitor to Britain, favouring open country. It will raid gardens to strip berried bushes in hard winters. Mistle Thrush is similar but is grey-brown above.

KNOT   winter 10 in (25 cm) passage migrant and winter visitor

Pale grey upperparts, head to tail. (Juvenile notably 'scaly' on back.)

◉ A stocky wader, grey and white, with a straight bill.

★ Forms huge flocks at specific coastal and estuary locations. Dunlin is similar, with longish, downcurved bill. The whiter Sanderling scuttles with waves. Both are notably smaller.

MISTLE THRUSH   10½ in (27 cm) resident

Upperparts a very grey-brown, unlike other thrushes of the region.

◉ Speckled breast, grey-brown upperparts and head.

★ Widespread. Very common on open parks and fields, needing trees for summer breeding. Song Thrush has orange-brown upperparts and orange 'wingpits'. Fieldfare has grey head and tail.

MERLIN   male 10½ in (27 cm) resident

Blue-grey above; crown, wings and body to tail (tipped black).

◉ Small bird of prey; pointed wings. Blue-grey above; faint moustache.

★ Uncommon. Favours upland, boggy and coast areas in north and west. Pursues prey with low-level dashing flight. Larger female is brown. Male Peregrine and Hobby have black heads and heavy moustaches.

WATER RAIL   11 in (28 cm) resident

Slate-grey face, throat, breast and upper belly.

◉ 'Chicken-shaped' with long bill.

★ Uncommon, secretive and restricted to reed beds and marshy areas with cover. You could spend a lifetime just missing this bird! But a glimpse of its bill separates it from a Moorhen.

GREY PLOVER   summer 11 in (28 cm) passage migrant

Dark silvery grey crown and upperparts. Back has 'scalloped' pattern.

◉ Extensive black underparts, black 'wingpits', whitish rump.

★ Visible in this plumage around coasts in spring and autumn. A stout bird, may be confused with summer Golden Plover (golden-brown back and rump). Dunlin has brown back and longish, downcurved bill.

GREY PLOVER   winter 11 in (28 cm) winter visitor

Drab brownish grey crown and upperparts. Breast has greyish brown streaking.

◉ Silvery grey upperparts with a white undivided rump. Black 'wingpits'.

★ On south and east coasts in winter. Stout, stubby-billed. Most confusion with slimmer Golden Plover (golden-brown back and rump), Knot and Dunlin (longer bills, white 'wingpits').

SPARROWHAWK   male 11 in (28 cm) resident

Blue-grey crown, upperwings and upperparts.

◉ Barred brick-red underparts. Grey back.

★ Widespread, reasonably common with numbers increasing. Round-tipped wings for hunting in woodland with dashing flight. Larger female has brown breast bars and back. Kestrel hovers.

SPOTTED REDSHANK   winter 12 in (30 cm) passage migrant and winter visitor

Crown and upperparts a fairly uniform pale grey.

◉ Long red legs, and white panel on back and rump (but not on wings).

★ Scarce, usually seen on coasts, or marshy areas inland. Confusion with brown-backed Redshank possible, but grey back will distinguish. Greenshank has greenish legs.

GREENSHANK   12 in (30 cm) summer visitor and passage migrant

Legs grey-green. Upperparts brownish grey. Head to side of breast grey.

◉ Long grey-green legs. Bill slightly upturned. White back 'V' in flight.

★ Uncommon breeding species in northern Scotland only. Mostly seen on passage at coasts, or inland water. More grey than the brown-backed Redshank. Beware similarity to red-legged winter Spotted Redshank.

PARTRIDGE   12 in (30 cm) resident

Grey on neck, breast, belly and flanks. 'Finger' of grey extends behind face.

👁 'Chicken-shaped', with orange-red face, grey neck and breast.

★ Quite common on agricultural land, often in small groups (coveys). Nervous, disturbs easily. Red-legged Partridge has white face and black 'necklace'; Pheasant is long-tailed.

COLLARED DOVE   12½ in (32 cm) resident

Pale bluish grey in wings and on belly.

👁 Black and white jagged collar mark.

★ Unknown in British Isles before 1952, this invader is now common and familiar in both gardens and farm buildings. Turtle Dove is very similar, but has 'scalloped' orange-brown back.

HOBBY   13 in (33 cm) summer visitor

Dark blue-grey upperparts and upperwings.

👁 Small bird of prey with pointed wings, red leggings and distinct moustache.

★ Very uncommon, breeding on southern heaths and open country. 'Hawks' agilely on insects and small birds. Robust adult Peregrine is similar, but barred grey below. Male Merlin has faint moustaches.

KESTREL   male 13 in (33 cm) resident

Plain pale grey head, rump and upper tail.

👁 Hovers repeatedly. Grey head and spotted brown back.

★ Easily the most numerous bird of prey in the region. Widespread and very visible hovering over prey. Female has brown, barred upperparts. Merlin, Peregrine and Sparrowhawk do not hover.

CUCKOO   adult 13 in (33 cm) summer visitor

Grey head, upperparts, upperwings and upper breast. Grey-barred below.

👁 The long, black, wedge-shaped tail has surprisingly obvious white spots.

★ Widespread, fairly common. Cuckoos are easy to hear, hard to find. They breed in many habitats, laying eggs in a variety of other species' nests. Male Sparrowhawk is brick-red below.

CUCKOO   juvenile 13 in (33 cm) summer visitor

These youngsters can be either grey-brown or red-brown above.

👁 The tail is long, brown, barred and wedge-shaped.

★ Widespread, fairly common, Cuckoos are easy to hear, hard to find. Their habitat varies with host parents' preferences. Female Sparrowhawk has banded tail, female Kestrel hovers.

STOCK DOVE   13 in (33 cm) resident

Mostly plain bluish grey, including rump.

👁 Very plain bluish grey pigeon-type, with black upperwing borders.

★ Fairly common in many habitats, only absent in far north. Often overlooked with other pigeon-types. Woodpigeon has wing flashes. Feral Pigeon has black underwing borders and double wingbars.

ROCK DOVE/FERAL PIGEON   13 in (33 cm) resident

Mostly pale grey, except as below.

👁 Town pigeon-type. White rump. Black double wing bars and underwing borders.

★ Feral Pigeons (Chequers, black and white, Fantail and racing strains) are widespread and common. True Rock Dove now only on north and west coasts. Stock Dove has black upperwing borders, grey rump.

'RED CHEQUER' FERAL PIGEON   13 in (33 cm) resident

Very pale grey tones in wings and some feather edges on back.

👁 Reddish and pale grey tones on a pigeon-type.

★ Feral Pigeons are very varied (Chequers, black/white, Fantail, racing strains), widespread and common in towns and on fields. Rock Dove ancestors now only found on north and west coasts.

JACKDAW   13 in (33 cm) resident

Light grey nape very visible. Darker grey on face, throat, breast and belly.

👁 Grey nape on a black bird. 'Chack' contact call.

★ A common bird, equally at ease around human habitation, in wooded areas, or on cliffs. Much smaller than Rook or Crow, its call is absolutely distinctive. Chough has red bill and legs.

COMMON TERN   13½ in (34 cm) summer visitor

Plain pale grey wings, back and rump.

◗ Forked tail, black tip to red bill, black cap.

★ Only moderately common, but breeds by inland water as well as on coasts, so highly visible. Arctic Tern very alike, but whole bill is blood-red. Black-headed Gull has brown head!

RED-LEGGED PARTRIDGE   13½ in (34 cm) resident

Grey on breast, and grey in flank streaks.

◗ Chicken-like shape, black 'necklace'.

★ An introduced species, now locally common in south and east England on agricultural land. Partridge has an orange-red face. Female Pheasant is all brown with a long tail.

TEAL   male 14 in (36 cm) resident

Grey on flanks, back and inner forewings (coverts).

◗ Chestnut head with dark green patch. Green and black speculum white-edged.

★ Widespread, rather uncommon breeding species, fond of rushy pools. Winter migrants swell numbers dramatically, forming groups on almost any body of water. Female is brown, with same speculum as male.

ARCTIC TERN   14½ in (37 cm) summer visitor

Plain pale grey wings and back. Underparts are a greyish white.

◗ Forked tail, blood-red bill, black cap.

★ Fairly common, but mainly restricted to northern coastal breeding sites. Common Tern is very similar, but red bill has black tip. Black-headed Gull has brown head!

BLACK-HEADED GULL   summer 14½ in (37 cm) resident

Pale grey wings (except for noticeable white wedge and black tips).

◗ Chocolate-brown 'hood' on head.

★ Common, the most visible inland gull. Breeds coastally, but also on inland marshy sites. Common and Arctic Terns are black-capped and have forked tails.

BLACK-HEADED GULL   winter 14½ in (37 cm) resident

Pale grey wings (except for noticeable white wedge and black tips).

◉ Prominent white wedge in outer wing. Reddish legs and bill. White tail.

★ Common, the most visible inland gull. Happily associates with man, seen at parks, fields and water sites. Common Gull has yellow legs and bill. Herring Gull has pink legs, yellow bill.

BLACK-HEADED GULL   immature 14½ in (37 cm) resident

Pale grey back, and grey areas in wings. Also grey patch on crown.

◉ Prominent white wedge in outer wing. Black band at tail tip.

★ Common, the most visible inland gull. Happily associates with man, seen at parks, fields and water sites. Immature Common and Herring Gulls have black tail tip, with all-dark outer wings.

BAR-TAILED GODWIT   winter 15 in (38 cm) passage migrant and winter visitor

Greyish brown upperparts, nape and crown. Back 'scalloped'.

◉ Medium-large wader. Long bill (slight upturn). White rump, no wing bars.

★ Uncommon, mainly seen on passage around coasts. Black-tailed Godwit has longer bill and legs and prominent white wing bars. Curlew and Whimbrel have long, downcurved bills.

PEREGRINE   male and female 15 in (38 cm) and 19 in (48 cm) respectively, resident

All upperparts blue-grey. Underwings barred with grey.

◉ Pointed wings, bold black moustaches. Incredible 'stooping' dive on to prey.

★ Was endangered, still uncommon. Robust falcon, with female larger than male. Juvenile is brown. Breeds on cliffs, inland or coastal. Hobby and Merlin more agile and delicate. Kestrel hovers.

BLACK-TAILED GODWIT   winter 15½ in (39 cm) passage migrant and winter visitor

Brownish grey upperparts, rather plain. Grey on head, neck and breast.

◉ Large wader. Long bill (appears straight). White rump and wing bar.

★ Regular winter visitor, commonest in south at estuaries and inland water. Bar-tailed Godwit has shorter legs and no wing bar. Curlew and Whimbrel have downcurved bills, no wing bars.

KITTIWAKE adult 16 in (41 cm) resident

Plain pale grey on back and most of upperwings.

◗ Yellow bill and black legs. 'Dipped-in-ink' wing tips seen in flight.

★ Perhaps surprisingly, the commonest British gull. Strictly maritime, it nests in colonies on cliffs, calling its name. Common Gull has yellow legs and white in wing tip.

KITTIWAKE juvenile 16 in (41 cm) resident

Plain pale grey on back and upperwings (with black 'W' overlaid).

◗ Black 'W'-mark on upperwings, black half-collar across neck. Black legs.

★ Perhaps surprisngly, the commonest British gull. Strictly maritime; may be overlooked for this reason. Calls its name at nesting colony. Immature Common Gull has brown in upperwing.

COMMON GULL adult 16 in (41 cm) resident

Pale grey back and upperwings. Head and nape greyish-streaked in winter.

◗ Pale grey back, yellow legs. Note white within black wing tips.

★ Not the commonest gull, but common inland and coastally. Northerly breeding on moors, lochs and fields. Herring Gull has pink legs, Kittiwake black legs, and winter Black-headed Gull red legs.

COMMON GULL immature (1st winter) 16 in (41 cm) resident

Pale grey back, and grey panels in upperwings. Grey-brown neck streaks.

◗ Grey back with brown, grey and black upperwings. Clear-cut black tail tip.

★ Common, inland and coastal. First-year Herring and Black-backed Gulls have less distinct tail bands, no grey in mid-upperwings. Immature Black-headed Gull has white wedges in outer wings.

SANDWICH TERN 16 in (41 cm) summer visitor

Very pale grey back and upperwings.

◗ Forked tail. Black bill with yellow tip. (Crested early in breeding season.)

★ The largest tern, rather uncommon, nesting in specific coastal colonies. Beware – crest lost in mid-summer. Other summer terns with white underparts have red or yellow bills and legs.

WOODPIGEON   16 in (41 cm) resident

Blue-grey head, lower back and rump. Wings and upper back browner.

👁 Prominent white wing flashes visible in flight at considerable distances.

★ Abundant and widespread, usually near trees, although it feeds in open. Other pigeons and doves lack the white wing flashes, but Feral Pigeon and Stock Dove might confuse when seen at rest in fields.

HEN HARRIER   male 17 in (43 cm) resident

Pale blue-grey head, upperwings, back and tail (but not rump).

👁 Low, slow, hunting flight. Grey tail and upperwings with a white rump.

★ Uncommon, with a northern and western breeding distribution. In winter visits fens, coasts and open country. Larger female, and both sexes of Marsh Harrier, have brown backs.

ROOK   18 in (46 cm) resident

Pale grey bare face and base of bill.

👁 Entirely black, with greyish white bare face and base of bill.

★ Common and gregarious, nesting high in tops of large trees in 'rookeries', usually near farmland. Carrion Crow has black-feathered face, Hooded Crow has grey body. Jackdaw has grey nape.

POCHARD   male 18 in (46 cm) resident

Pale grey wings, back and flanks. Paler grey wing bar (obscure).

👁 Reddish brown head, black breast, grey back.

★ Not very common breeding species, but widespread, mostly on lakes. Winter migrants swell numbers at reservoirs, lakes, etc. Female mostly brownish. Female Goldeneye has grey breast.

POCHARD   female 18 in (46 cm) resident

Back, wings and flanks a brownish grey. Obscure pale grey wing bar.

👁 Dark brown breast and greyish flanks. In flight, obscure grey wing bar.

★ Not very common breeding species, but widespread, mostly on lakes. Winter migrants swell numbers at reservoirs, lakes, etc. Compare with female Tufted Duck; brown back and flanks, white wing bars.

GOLDENEYE   female 18 in (46 cm) winter visitor

Grey back, breast and flanks.

◐ Grey back, whole head plain brown. Nearly all of inner wing white.

★ Uncommon, sea and freshwater duck. Immature is duller, with no yellow bill tip. Male has green head, white face spot. Male Goosander and Merganser are a different shape. Male Wigeon has forehead blaze.

WIGEON   male 18 in (46 cm) mainly a winter visitor

Pale grey back and flanks.

◐ Yellowish blaze down the crown and forehead. White inner forewing.

★ A common winter visitor, flocking on large water bodies, the sea and coastal grasslands. Also a passage migrant and scarce breeding species. Female Goldeneye has a white collar.

HOODED CROW   18½ in (47 cm) resident

Plain grey body.

◐ Medium-large size. Grey body with black wings.

★ Both Crows are very common, usually favouring open country with trees. Hooded Crow is found throughout Ireland, north and west Scotland. (Carrion Crow is the same species.)

FULMAR   18½ in (47 cm) resident

Back, upperwings and tail are pale grey. Outer wings rather darker.

◐ Tube-nose (if seen). Bull neck; stiff wings in flight; quite unlike gulls.

★ A sea-going species, once scarce, now common around coasts. A cliff-nester. Clumsy on land, but a complete master of the air. Grey gulls and terns show black in wings, or on head.

MARSH HARRIER   male 19 in (48 cm) variable status

Grey outer wings and tail. Very dark grey in wing tips.

◐ Low, slow, hunting flight. Brown body with grey in wings.

★ A very scarce species, with migrants and the small breeding population both being irregular in numbers. Female Marsh Harrier virtually all brown. Hen Harrier has white rump.

GADWALL   male 20 in (51 cm) resident and winter visitor

Appears mostly grey. Flanks, breast and upper back are all darkish grey.

👁 Greyest-looking duck, with prominent white patch near sitting bird's tail.

★ Scarce breeding species, augmented by winter visitors. Prefers slow-moving fresh water. Brown female shows orange on bill, prominent in good light. Male Wigeon has yellow blaze on head.

LESSER BLACK-BACKED GULL   adult 21 in (53 cm) resident

Back and upperwings plain grey, but can vary from dark to medium.

👁 Back and wings are dark grey (can vary in intensity); yellow legs.

★ Fairly common, breeds on level sites around coasts, but also inland. Pink-legged Herring Gull very similar to the palest Lessers. Much larger Great Black-backed also has pink legs.

HERRING GULL   adult 22 in (56 cm) resident

Back and upperwings are plain pale grey.

👁 Light grey back and wings, pink legs.

★ Common around most coasts, breeds on cliffs and dunes, venturing inland more in winter. Common Gull and the palest Lesser Black-backed have yellowish legs; Kittiwake has black legs.

RED-BREASTED MERGANSER   male 23 in (58 cm) resident

Darkish grey flanks, rump and tail. Forewings also grey.

👁 Green head shows double crest. White speculum and inner wing. 'Saw'-billed.

★ Rather uncommon. Breeds in north and west near water; includes sites far inland. Sea-going in winter. Male Goosander is white-bodied. Male Mallard has dark inner wing and blue speculum.

RED-BREASTED MERGANSER   female 23 in (58 cm) resident

Mostly grey. Includes chin, most of body and tail. Slightly darker above.

👁 Chestnut head has double crest. Pale throat. White speculum. 'Saw'-billed.

★ Rather uncommon. Breeds in north and west near water; includes sites far inland. Sea-going in winter. Female Goosander has smoother crest, and dark neck contrasts with pale breast.

BRENT GOOSE   23 in (58 cm) winter visitor

Upperparts are dark brownish grey. Belly similar (or whitish).

◑ Smallest and darkest goose, with whole of head black.

★ Large, highly visible winter flocks gather at southerly estuarine and coastal field locations. Otherwise sea-going. Barnacle and Canada Geese are dark-necked, but have white on faces.

BARNACLE GOOSE   25 in (64 cm) winter visitor

Lot of grey visible in folded wings and lower back. Some grey flank streaks.

◑ Goose with white face and grey back.

★ Only common at favoured sites on north and west coastal grasslands, where they may gather in thousands. Canada Goose has white 'chinstrap'. Brent Goose has white neck patch. Both are brown-backed.

GOOSANDER   female 26 in (66 cm) resident

Grey flanks, upper body and tail. Grey forewings.

◑ Chestnut head, smooth crest obscure. Neck/breast contrast. 'Saw'-billed.

★ Rather uncommon. Northerly breeding, normally by fresh water. More widely spread in winter. Female Merganser is very similar, but note spiky double crest; pale throat lacks contrasts.

PINTAIL   male 26 in (66 in) winter visitor

Mostly medium grey; flanks, upper back, forewing, rump and tail base.

◑ Long pointed tail. 'Finger' of white rising from breast into dark head.

★ Mainly rather uncommon winter visitor to coasts and estuaries. Also a scarce breeding species. Some similarity to darker-breasted, yellow-crowned Wigeon, but only at long distances.

GREYLAG GOOSE   33 in (84 cm) resident

Most of plumage is blend of brown and grey. Overall, mainly grey.

◑ Large grey-brown goose, with a plain orange bill and pink legs.

★ Uncommon breeding species, but winter numbers swollen by migrants. Often seen at marshes and wet grassland. Brent, Barnacle and Canada Geese all have black necks and bills.

GREY HERON   35 in (89 cm) resident

Hindneck and whole of upper body grey. Forewings grey in flight.

👁 Extremely long neck (folded back in flight). Grey back.

★ Not numerically common at all, but a big bird, often out in the open and highly visible. Builds platform nests in tree tops, often in colonies (can get very noisy!). Bittern similar, but very brown.

MUTE SWAN   juvenile 38 in (97 cm) resident

'Dirty' grey-brown tones. Grey bill and darker legs. (Downy young are grey.)

👁 Largest and heaviest bird of the region. Whole bird a 'dirty' white.

★ Widespread, reasonably common, and very, very visible. Normally in the company of parents, which are all white with red bills. Preference for slow-moving water.

GOLDCREST 3½ in (9 cm) resident

Black crown stripes. Black in wings.

◉ Tiny, active bird (smallest of region), greenish with orange crown.

★ Widespread. Very common in coniferous woodland, also gardens and other woodland. Might just be confused with small warblers (no wing bars or crown stripes), or tits (whitish cheeks).

COAL TIT 4½ in (11 cm) resident

Head black, except for white cheeks and nape.

◉ Obvious white nape stripe.

★ They require trees, mostly conifers, where they are very common and widespread. Most alike are Willow and Marsh Tits, which have black napes and plain wings.

CRESTED TIT 4½ in (11 cm) resident

Head black and white.

◉ Obvious black and white crest.

★ In Britain they are located only in coniferous forests of northern Scotland, where they are locally common. Possible confusion with black-capped Coal Tit.

MARSH TIT 4½ in (11 cm) resident

Glossy black cap. Black chin.

◉ Glossy black cap, no wing bars or patches, and often-used 'pitchu' call.

★ Fairly common woodland species, restricted mainly to England and Wales. Willow Tit is very similar, but has a pale wing patch and gives 'eee' calls.

WILLOW TIT 4½ in (11 cm) resident

Dull black cap and chin patch.

◉ Dull black cap, pale wing patch, main call a sequence of 'eee's.

★ Fairly uncommon woodland species, breeding mainly in England and Wales. Marsh Tit is very similar, but has unmarked wings and gives 'pitchu' call.

SISKIN   male 4½ in (11 cm) resident and winter visitor

Black forehead and chin. Black in wings and on tail, streaks on flanks.

👁 Streaked black, green and yellow bird, with a black forehead and chin.

★ Fairly common winter visitor, notably at garden peanut bags. Small breeding populations in coniferous woodlands, especially in Scotland. Female is plainer-faced. Beware similarity to unstreaked Greenfinch.

SISKIN   female 4½ in (11 cm) resident and winter visitor

Whole bird prominently streaked with black. Black in wings and on tail.

👁 Streaked black, green and yellow bird, with plain chin and striped crown.

★ Fairly common winter visitor, notably at peanut bags. Breeds in coniferous woodland locally, especially in Scotland. Male has black forehead and chin. Beware similarity to unstreaked Greenfinch.

GOLDFINCH   adult 4¾ in (12 cm) resident

Black on head, wings and tail.

👁 Red, white and black head pattern.

★ Common and widespread (except in north Scotland), found on both open ground and in gardens. They love thistle seeds. Head pattern eliminates confusion with other species.

GOLDFINCH   juvenile 4¾ in (12 cm) resident

Black on wings and tail.

👁 Single broad, brilliant yellow wing bars, with the head streaked brown.

★ Common and widespread (except in north Scotland), found on both open ground and in gardens. They love thistle seeds. The Siskin is similar, but shows double yellow wing bars and is clearly greenish.

REDPOLL   male (both adults similar) 5 in (13 cm) resident

Black chin.

👁 Crimson forehead and black chin.

★ Reasonably common, but easy to miss. Often in large acrobatic flocks, they require trees, from heaths to conifer plantations. The adult male Linnet has a crimson forehead with a whitish chin.

SEDGE WARBLER 5 in (13 cm) summer visitor

Thin black eye and crown stripes. Heavily striped upper back.

◉ Very prominent whitish stripe over eye, with a black-streaked crown.

★ Common in reeds and other thick cover near water. Notable for loud churring song. Widespread across British Isles all summer. Compare Reed Warbler's plain plumage and faint eye stripe.

STONECHAT male 5 in (13 cm) resident

Entirely black-hooded head. Black markings in back and wings.

◉ Entirely black head with prominent white neck patch.

★ Widely present, but with a markedly western distribution. A bird of open country, frequently seen atop a gorse bush. Female and juvenile are duller and more streaked, as is Whinchat.

PIED FLYCATCHER male 5 in (13 cm) summer visitor

All head and upperparts black, except for forehead and prominent wing bars.

◉ Black and white plumage only, with conspicuous white wing bar.

★ Uncommon. Seen mainly on passage, or at favoured woodland sites, usually deciduous (and mostly in Wales). A hole-nesting species, it readily takes to nest boxes. No look-alikes.

HOUSE MARTIN 5 in (13 cm) summer visitor

Appears all black above (apart from rump).

◉ Swallow-type bird with a white rump.

★ Common and widespread. Originally a bird of open country. Now associated with man, building mud nests under house eaves. Sand Martin is similar with obvious brown breast bar, no white rump.

LITTLE STINT juvenile 5 in (13 cm) passage migrant

Legs are black.

◉ Tiny (smallest wader in the region), with a short, straight bill.

★ Rather uncommon, seen mainly on autumn passage, usually by inland water. Beware superficial resemblance to juvenile Dunlin (twice as bulky, longer downcurved bill).

LONG-TAILED TIT   5½ in (14 cm) resident

Black above eye, on nape, in back and wings, and full length of tail.

👁 Tiny bird with pink in plumage, and a disproportionately long tail.

★ Almost never on ground, they require trees or bushes, even if sparse. Numerous and widespread, forming small flocks outside breeding season. (Beware some similarity to ground-loving Pied Wagtail.)

BLACKCAP   male 5½ in (14 cm) summer visitor

Black cap.

👁 Clear cut black cap, grey face and breast.

★ Common summer visitor, scarcest in Scotland and Ireland. Requires trees or scrub. Female has reddish brown cap. Possible confusion with Marsh and Willow Tits, but note their whitish cheeks.

REDSTART   male 5½ in (14 cm) summer visitor

Black face and throat.

👁 Reddish brown tail, frequently flicked. Obvious white forehead.

★ Widespread, but local and not very common. Preferred habitats are mature woods, or more open country with good cover. A very distinctive bird, with no look-alikes.

BLACK REDSTART   male 5½ in (14 cm) summer visitor

Very sooty appearance overall. Face, throat and breast blackest.

👁 Very dark plumage, with frequently flicked, reddish brown tail.

★ A rare breeding bird to the British Isles, it is a ground-loving species. Often nests in cities in old walls or buildings. The drab female is browner and lacks the white wing patch.

GREAT TIT   5½ in (14 cm) resident

Head is black with white cheeks. Very obvious black stripe from chin to belly.

👁 Black stripe from chin to belly (broader on male bird).

★ A very common bird, found wherever trees and hedgerows occur, and a familiar garden species. The smaller, blue-headed Blue Tit also has a belly stripe, but fainter and blue-grey.

TREE SPARROW 5½ in (14 cm) resident

Black chin and small bib, black cheek spot. Black streaking on upper back.

◑ Chocolate-brown crown, black cheek spot.

★ Increasingly local nowadays in its more traditional open country haunts, it is most likely to be mistaken for the grey-crowned male House Sparrow.

NUTHATCH 5½ in (14 cm) resident

Black 'bandit's' mask. Black in tail feathers.

◑ Climbs about tree trunks in any direction. Blue-grey upperparts.

★ Reasonably common throughout Wales and southern England, invariably associated with trunks of trees. Treecreeper shares habitat, but is mainly brown and only ascends trunks.

HOUSE SPARROW male 5¾ in (14.5 cm) resident

Black throat and bib. Upperparts streaked with black.

◑ Grey crown, black bib.

★ Widespread and abundant, but prefers town areas and farm buildings. Female is rather nondescript, with clear pale eye stripe. Tree Sparrow is similar, but has black cheek spot, chocolate-brown crown.

WHEATEAR male 5¾ in (14.5 cm) summer visitor

Blackish wings. Black inverted 'T' on tail. Black mask.

◑ Black inverted 'T' on the white tail. Grey crown and back.

★ Reasonably common, and very visible in western and northern regions. Likes wide open spaces – cliff tops, moors, bare uplands. Female and Whinchat have brown heads and backs.

WHEATEAR female 5¾ in (14.5 cm) summer visitor

Brownish black inverted 'T' on tail.

◑ Dark inverted 'T' on the white tail. Brown crown and back.

★ Reasonably common, and very visible in western and northern regions. Likes wide open spaces – cliff tops, moors and bare uplands. Male has grey back, Whinchat streaked back.

BULLFINCH   male 5¾ in (14.5 cm) resident

Black cap, wings and tail.

👁 White rump, bright pink breast.

★ Common and widespread, they are found in woods and gardens. Noted as an orchard pest due to their liking for buds. Female and juvenile are brown-breasted, the latter without the cap.

BULLFINCH   female and juvenile 5¾ in (14.5 cm) resident

Black cap, wings and tail.

👁 White rump, plain brown breast. (Juvenile lacks female's black cap.)

★ Common and widespread, they are found in woods and gardens. Noted as an orchard pest due to their liking for buds. The male has a bright pink breast. Young birds lack black cap.

LESSER SPOTTED WOODPECKER   6 in (15 cm) resident

Upperparts mainly black, spotted with white. Black moustache, wings and tail.

👁 White-barred back ('skeleton's bones'!). Male only has red crown.

★ Uncommon, restricted to southern Britain, and found in well-timbered habitats. Great Spotted Woodpecker is similar, but has obvious white 'shoulder-blades' and is nearly the size of a Blackbird.

BRAMBLING   winter 6 in (15 cm) winter visitor

Prominent black in wings. Blackish on tail, and markings on upper back.

👁 White rump, orange breast.

★ Rather uncommon, fluctuating numbers arrive from September onwards. Beech woods are a favourite location, but they are seen in open fields also. Chaffinch is similar, but has a green rump.

REED BUNTING   male 6 in (15 cm) resident

Head hooded in black (split by the white moustachial stripe).

👁 White moustache through black hood. (Hood browner in autumn and winter.)

★ Common and widespread, breeding near wet areas. At other times may be seen in fields or gardens. Often chooses to perch prominently. The female is much browner-headed.

103

170

LITTLE RINGED PLOVER   6 in (15 cm) summer visitor

Black forehead and mask. Black collar encircles neck and upper breast.

👁 Complete black breast band, and absence of any visible wing bar.

★ Uncommon summer visitor (and only to England), but very visible at gravel pits and other freshwater breeding sites. Slightly larger Ringed Plover shares breast bar, but has wing bar also.

BEARDED TIT   male 6½ in (17 cm) resident

'Drooping' black moustaches. Some black in forewings and on undertail.

👁 Black 'drooping moustaches'.

★ Very scarce. Restricted to reed bed breeding habitats, mainly coastal, and mainly in East Anglia. (Remote possibility of confusion with black, white and pink Long-tailed Tit.)

YELLOW WAGTAIL   6½ in (17 cm) summer visitor

Black inner tail. Some black in wings.

👁 Repeated tail-wagging, combined with yellowish green back colouring.

★ Rather uncommon, preferring meadow and marshy breeding conditions, mostly restricted to England and Wales. Grey Wagtail is very yellow, but has grey face and extremely long tail.

SNOW BUNTING   winter male (both adults similar) 6½ in (17 cm) winter visitor

Black wing tips. Black inner tail.

👁 Plumage is very variable, but large amount of white always distinctive.

★ A very rare breeding species, normally seen as a scarce winter visitor to eastern coasts and inland hills. Flocks form in winter, looking like 'a flurry of snowflakes'.

SWIFT   6½ in (17 cm) summer visitor

Apparently all black (actually dark brown with a pale throat!).

👁 Circles above continually on scythe-shaped wings. Apparently all black.

★ Common visitor to British Isles, only absent in parts of northern Scotland. Often nests under eaves of buildings. House Martin is stockier, with white rump. Swallow has long tail streamers.

PIED WAGTAIL summer male 7 in (18 cm) resident

Black bib. Black upperparts from crown to wings, rump and inner tail.

👁 Long tail, repeatedly wagged. Black and white plumage, with a black back.

★ Very common and highly visible in virtually all habitats. 'Tizzik' call given from an undulating flight. Summer females, and both sexes in winter, have grey backs.

PIED WAGTAIL summer female and both sexes in winter 7 in (18 cm) resident

Black bib, crown, rump and inner tail. Some black in wings.

👁 Long tail, repeatedly wagged. Black and white plumage, dark grey back.

★ Very common, highly visible in almost all habitats. 'Tizzik' call from an undulating flight. Summer female has black bib which diminishes in winter. Summer male has black bib and back.

PIED WAGTAIL juvenile 7 in (18 cm) resident

Rather grubby black on bib and around face. Black on wings, rump and tail.

👁 Long tail, repeatedly wagged. Brownish grey upperparts.

★ Very common and highly visible in virtually all habitats. 'Tizzik' call given from undulating flight. Adults have white faces.

GREY WAGTAIL summer male 7 in (18 cm) resident

Bold black throat. Black in wings and inner tail.

👁 Extreme length of tail, repeatedly wagged. Grey face, black throat.

★ Widespread, reasonably common. Almost always close to fast-running streams. Female and winter male white-throated. Yellow Wagtail has yellowish green back. Pied Wagtail, no yellow at all.

GREY WAGTAIL summer female and both sexes in winter 7 in (18 cm) resident

Black in wings and inner tail.

👁 Extreme length of tail, repeatedly wagged. Grey face, white throat.

★ Widespread, reasonably common. Almost always close to fast-running streams. Summer male has black throat. Yellow Wagtail has yellowish green back. Pied Wagtail, no yellow at all.

HAWFINCH   7 in (18 cm) resident

Black bib. Upperwings mostly black, underwings black-edged (seen in flight).

👁 Oversized bill, and white underwing markings (white, bordered black).

★ Widely spread, but distinctly scarce and secretive in its wooded habitat. Not as visible as Chaffinch with its obvious white outer tail feathers, or Bullfinch with white rump.

WAXWING   7 in (18 cm) winter visitor

Black throat, mask, wing tips and broad band on tail.

👁 Red 'wax' in inner wing, crest and yellow tail tip are all unmistakable.

★ A distinctly scarce visitor. Small groups turn up in variable numbers in unpredictable locations, almost always on berried bushes. Could just be mistaken for Starling in flight.

DUNLIN   summer 7½ in (19 cm) resident

Black belly patch. Rich brown and black back markings. Black legs.

👁 Black belly patch, downcurved bill.

★ Rather uncommon breeding bird, limited to northern moorland. Passage birds often retain black belly. In summer Golden and Grey Plovers are also black below, but have short, stubby bills.

RINGED PLOVER   adult 7½ in (19 cm) resident

Black forehead, mask and on wings. Black collar encirlces neck and upper breast.

👁 Complete black breast band. White wing bar obvious in flight.

★ Breeds widely around coasts. Also a common winter sight on estuaries. Juvenile bird has partial breast band. Little Ringed Plover lacks wing bar. Dunlin is only similar in flight.

SANDERLING   winter 8 in (20 cm) passage migrant and winter visitor

Black on wings. Black legs.

👁 Remarkable scuttling runs at edge of waves.

★ Not common, and almost exclusively seen on sandy coastlines in winter. Dunlin may cause confusion, but has a longer, slightly downcurved bill, and a 'stitching' feeding technique.

STARLING   adult 8½ in (22 cm) resident

Can appear all black, or show a colourful 'oily' gloss in good light.

👁 Glossy summer plumage (speckled in winter). Pointed wings seen in flight.

★ Abundant. Forms huge noisy flocks before roosting in cities or country cover. Juvenile birds are a plain 'mouse-brown'. Not likely to be confused with any other common bird.

GREAT SPOTTED WOODPECKER   9 in (23 cm) resident

Upperparts mainly black, with white markings. Black in underwings also.

👁 White 'shoulder' patches.

★ Widespread, it is the commonest British woodpecker. Dependent on trees and hedgerows. Lesser Spotted Woodpecker is similar, but uncommon and only sparrow-sized.

GREEN SANDPIPER   9 in (23 cm) passage migrant

Appears black and white in flight. (If view is good, seen as dark brown and white.)

👁 Dark back contrasts with white rump. (Appears black and white in flight.)

★ Uncommon migrant, seen at reservoirs, lakes and sewage farms. A few overwinter in southern England. Common Sandpiper has 'saddle' mark on neck. Redshank and Greenshank are larger and leggier.

TURNSTONE   summer 9 in (23 cm) passage migrant

Unique black breast and head pattern. Black on back and tail (pied in flight).

👁 'Tortoiseshell' back plumage, white on head.

★ Seen on passage around rocky coasts, usually very well-camouflaged. Summer dark-headed, dark-backed Purple Sandpiper should not confuse. Ringed Plover prefers sand and pebbles.

RUFF   female and winter male 9 in (23 cm) and 12 in (30 cm) respectively, passage migrant

Black centres to individual back feathers produce 'scalloped' effect.

👁 'Scalloped' brownish grey upperparts, and prominent divided white rump.

★ Small parties usually seen on passage on wetland habitat inland. Greenshank and Redshank show plain white rump and lower back in flight. Golden Plover in flight shows no white on rump.

LITTLE TERN   9½ in (24 cm) summer visitor

Yellow bill has black tip. Black eye stripe and crown. Black wing tips.

👁 Forked tail, and yellow bill with a black tip.

★ An uncommon and vulnerable seabird, breeding locally on shingle and sandy coasts. Small size distinctive, but note much larger Sandwich Tern's bill is black with a yellow tip.

BLACK TERN   summer 9½ in (24 cm) passage migrant

Black head and body, back becoming paler towards the rump.

👁 Forked tail and black body.

★ Rather uncommon, usually seen in small groups on passage at lakes, reservoirs, etc. Buoyant flight and black body identify in spring (but beware autumn juveniles – white-bodied!).

RING OUZEL   male 9½ in (24 cm) summer visitor

All black bird, except for white crescent on upper breast.

👁 Clean white crescent on a black bird.

★ Quite uncommon, appears rare due to inaccessible breeding grounds on high moors in north and west Britain. Male Blackbird is similar (especially partial albinos, which often occurs in Blackbirds).

BLACKBIRD   male 10 in (25 cm) resident

All black bird.

👁 All black bird, except for bill (yellow on adult, dark on juvenile).

★ Found throughout the region, truly abundant. A woodland bird, now familiar in any back garden. Partial albinos are common, so beware those like Ring Ouzel (white breast crescent).

SNIPE   10½ in (27 cm) resident

Black stripes on crown, through eye and down back. Black in wings and on tail.

👁 Flushes noisily, giving 'scaap' call in zig-zag flight.

★ Common and widespread, it is a bird of wet habitats in open country. Often the first indication of the bird is the explosive take-off. Woodcock is larger woodland bird.

TURTLE DOVE   10½ in (27 cm) summer visitor

Black in neck patch and 'scalloped' back. Dark wing tips and on tail.

◉ Neck patch. 'Scalloped' orange-brown outer back and inner wings.

★ Fairly common in the south and east, associated with trees and cultivated land. Song is a soft 'purring'. Collared Dove has a plain brown back and harsh song. Stock Dove has no white.

GOLDEN PLOVER   summer 11 in (28 cm) resident (the northern form is illustrated)

Black on face, down to breast and belly. Black legs. Black and gold back.

◉ Varying amounts of black on belly; stubby bill; golden-brown upperparts.

★ Not very common, and easily missed on inaccessible, northerly upland moors. More visible on passage. Grey Plover is bulkier and silvery grey above. Ruff has white belly and divided white rump.

GREY PLOVER   summer 11 in (28 cm) passage migrant

Black on face, down neck to breast and belly. Black legs. Black and silver back.

◉ Extensive black underparts, black 'wingpits', whitish rump.

★ Visible in this plumage around coasts in spring and autumn. A stout bird, may be confused with summer Golden Plover (golden-brown back and rump). Dunlin has brown back and longish, downcurved bill.

GREY PLOVER   winter 11 in (28 cm) winter visitor

Black 'wingpits'. Blackish legs.

◉ Silvery grey upperparts with a white undivided rump. Black 'wingpits'.

★ On south and east coasts in winter. Stout, stubby-billed. Most confusion with slimmer Golden Plover (golden-brown back and rump), Knot and Dunlin (longer bills, white 'wingpits').

SPOTTED REDSHANK   summer 11 in (28 cm) passage migrant

Virtually all black (except for white speckles and back panel, red legs).

◉ Body almost completely black.

★ Scarce, with summer plumage most visible on northerly migration in May. Seen on coasts, or marshy areas inland. Redshank and Greenshank are both much paler.

RUFF   summer male 12 in (30 cm) passage migrant
Varied amounts of black in ear-tufts and ruff. Dark centre to tail.

👁 Extraordinary ruff and ear-tufts.

★ Rare British breeding bird, limited to a few wet meadows and marshy sites. Greenshank and Redshank have undivided white rumps and lower backs. At a distance Golden Plover shows brown rump.

LAPWING   12 in (30 cm) resident
Black crest, chin, bib, wing tips and tail tip. Green back appears black.

👁 Crest, and flapping flight.

★ Common and widespread, a familiar bird of farmland and open ground. 'Pee-wit' call gives the bird its country name. At a distance, golden-brown Golden Plover might appear similar.

PUFFIN   summer 12 in (30 cm) resident
All upperparts black. Black crown and collar.

👁 Multi-coloured triangular bill. At a distance, note whirring wing action.

★ Fairly common, visiting off-shore islands to breed in summer. Bill distinguishes it from larger relatives, Razorbill and Guillemot. (Note that bill is smaller on winter adult and juvenile.)

COLLARED DOVE   12½ in (32 cm) resident
Black in neck patch. Dark tips to upperwings. Black base to undertail.

👁 Black and white jagged collar mark.

★ Unknown in British Isles before 1952, this invader is now common and familiar in both gardens and farm buildings. Turtle Dove is very similar, but has 'scalloped' orange-brown back.

HOBBY   13 in (33 cm) summer visitor
Head has black crown and moustaches. Underparts streaked with black.

👁 Small bird of prey with pointed wings, red leggings and distinct moustache.

★ Very uncommon, breeding on southern heaths and open country. 'Hawks' agilely on insects and small birds. Robust adult Peregrine is similar, but barred grey below. Male Merlin has faint moustaches.

KESTREL   male 13 in (33 cm) resident

Black wing tips, tail band, spots above and streaks below. Thin black moustache.

👁 Hovers repeatedly. Grey head and spotted brown back.

★ Easily the most numerous bird of prey in the region. Widespread and very visible hovering over prey. Female has brown, barred upperparts. Merlin, Peregrine and Sparrowhawk do not hover.

STOCK DOVE   13 in (33 cm) resident

Black upperwing borders, two partial wing bars and tail tip.

👁 Very plain bluish grey pigeon-type, with black upperwing borders.

★ Fairly common in many habitats, only absent in far north. Often overlooked with other pigeon-types. Woodpigeon has wing flashes. Feral Pigeon has black underwing borders and double wingbars.

ROCK DOVE/FERAL PIGEON   13 in (33 cm) resident

Black underwing borders, two wing bars, tail tip. (Some Ferals are all black.)

👁 Town pigeon-type. White rump. Black double wing bars and underwing borders.

★ Feral Pigeons (Chequers, black and white, Fantail and racing strains) are widespread and common. True Rock Dove now only on north and west coasts. Stock Dove has black upperwing borders, grey rump.

JACKDAW   13 in (33 cm) resident

Can appear all black, especially in silhouette (but look for grey nape).

👁 Grey nape on a black bird. 'Chack' contact call.

★ A common bird, equally at ease around human habitation, in wooded areas, or on cliffs. Much smaller than Rook or Crow, its call is absolutely distinctive. Chough has red bill and legs.

MOORHEN   13 in (33 cm) resident

Can appear all black (with flank stripes), but upperparts quite brown.

👁 White flank stripes, red frontal shield over bill.

★ Common and widespread where there are freshwater sites with cover. Easily alarmed; undertail flashes warning. Coot has white frontal shield and plain flanks. Water Rail has long bill.

11

COMMON TERN   13½ in (34 cm) summer visitor

Black cap. Some black edging to wing tips.

👁 Forked tail, black tip to red bill, black cap.

★ Only moderately common, but breeds by inland water as well as on coasts, so highly visible. Arctic Tern very alike, but whole bill is blood-red. Black-headed Gull has brown head!

BLACK GUILLEMOT   summer 13½ in (34 cm) resident

All black, except for wing patches and feet.

👁 Pure white wing patch, red feet.

★ Locally fairly common, mainly around north and west coasts. Guillemot and Razorbill are plain dark above, but beware similarity to Eider in late summer plumage, seen at a distance out at sea.

RED-LEGGED PARTRIDGE   13½ in (34 cm) resident

Black margins to white cheeks, black 'necklace', black in flank streaks.

👁 Chicken-like shape, black 'necklace'.

★ An introduced species, now locally common in south and east England on agricultural land. Partridge has an orange-red face. Female Pheasant is all brown with a long tail.

WOODCOCK   13½ in (34 cm) resident

Black bars on head. Upperparts blend black in with brown. Black on tail.

👁 The only long-billed bird normally associated with woodland.

★ Widespread and not uncommon, but very difficult to spot on the ground. Usually seen as brown blur exploding from cover, or in circular display flight. Smaller Snipe prefers wet open areas.

KESTREL   female 14 in (36 cm) resident

Black wing tips, tail band, bars above and streaks below. Thin black moustache.

👁 Hovers repeatedly. Upper body barred.

★ Easily the most numerous bird of prey in the region. Widespread and very visible hovering over prey. Male has grey head and spotted back. Merlin, Peregrine and Sparrowhawk do not hover.

JAY   14 in (36 cm) resident

Black in crest and wings. Moustache and all of tail black.

◉ Brilliant blue wing patches.

★ Common and widespread where there are trees; absent from far north. Quite shy, but bright colouring and raucous calls make this the most spectacular member of the crow family.

MANX SHEARWATER   14 in (36 cm) summer visitor

All upperparts black, crown to tail tip. Underwings black-edged.

◉ Black and white tube-nosed seabird. Tilting flight low over the water.

★ Surprisingly numerous, but hard to observe, as it breeds on off-shore islands which it visits at night. Visible during daylight, off coasts. Tube-nosed Fulmar is grey and white.

ARCTIC TERN   14½ in (37 cm) summer visitor

Black cap. Some black edging to wing tips.

◉ Forked tail, blood-red bill, black cap.

★ Fairly common, but mainly restricted to northern coastal breeding sites. Common Tern is very similar, but red bill has black tip. Black-headed Gull has brown head!

BLACK-HEADED GULL   immature 14½ in (37 cm) resident

'Smudge' behind eye. Black in wing tips. Black tail band.

◉ Prominent white wedge in outer wing. Black band at tail tip.

★ Common, the most visible inland gull. Happily associates with man, seen at parks, fields and water sites. Immature Common and Herring Gulls have black tail tip, with all-dark outer wings.

CHOUGH   15 in (38 cm) resident

All black, except for bill and legs.

◉ All black, except for red bill and legs.

★ Scarcest of the crow family, having suffered a steady decline in numbers. Restricted to sea cliffs in west and south, commonest in Ireland. Bill distinguishes it from Jackdaw and Crow.

BAR-TAILED GODWIT   winter 15 in (38 cm) passage migrant and winter visitor

Dark bars on tail tips, dark legs.

👁 Medium-large wader. Long bill (slight upturn). White rump, no wing bars.

★ Uncommon, mainly seen on passage around coasts. Black-tailed Godwit has longer bill and legs and prominent white wing bars. Curlew and Whimbrel have long, downcurved bills.

PEREGRINE   male and female 15 in (38 cm) and 19 in (48 cm) respectively, resident

Much of head black, with moustaches. Black bars below, and on tail.

👁 Pointed wings, bold black moustaches. Incredible 'stooping' dive on to prey.

★ Was endangered, still uncommon. Robust falcon, with female larger than male. Juvenile is brown. Breeds on cliffs, inland or coastal. Hobby and Merlin more agile and delicate. Kestrel hovers.

PEREGRINE   juvenile 15–19 in (38–48 cm) resident

Much of head blackish, with moustaches. Dark streaking below.

👁 Pointed wings, bold brown moustaches. Incredible 'stooping' dive on to prey.

★ Was endangered and is still unusual. Robust falcon, adults with blue-grey backs. Outside breeding season it favours most open habitats. Hobby and Merlin are more agile and delicate; Kestrel hovers.

COOT   15 in (38 cm) resident

All black (except for frontal shield and bill).

👁 White frontal shield over bill.

★ Common and highly visible on most large bodies of fresh water. Gregarious in winter, sometimes in gatherings of hundreds. Moorhen has flank stripes and red frontal shield.

SHORT-EARED OWL   15 in (38 cm) resident

Very dark mid-wing patches prominent. Upperparts mottled with black.

👁 Ground-loving, daytime-hunting owl of rough open country (rarely farmland).

★ Quite scarce, restricted to rough and open country away from interference. Highest densities in northern England and Scotland, absent from Ireland. It is the only owl likely in this habitat.

BLACK-TAILED GODWIT   winter 15½ in (39 cm) passage migrant and winter visitor

Black tail band. Dark legs. Dark upperwing contrasts with wing bar.

👁 Large wader. Long bill (appears straight). White rump and wing bar.

★ Regular winter visitor, commonest in south at estuaries and inland water. Bar-tailed Godwit has shorter legs and no wing bar. Curlew and Whimbrel have downcurved bills, no wing bars.

KITTIWAKE   adult 16 in (41 cm) resident

Black 'dipped-in-ink' wing tips. Black legs.

👁 Yellow bill and black legs. 'Dipped-in-ink' wing tips seen in flight.

★ Perhaps surprisingly, the commonest British gull. Strictly maritime, it nests in colonies on cliffs, calling its name. Common Gull has yellow legs and white in wing tip.

KITTIWAKE   juvenile 16 in (41 cm) resident

Black 'W'-mark on upperwings, 'ear' spot, half-collar, tail tip and legs.

👁 Black 'W'-mark on upperwings, black half-collar across neck. Black legs.

★ Perhaps surprisngly, the commonest British gull. Strictly maritime; may be overlooked for this reason. Calls its name at nesting colony. Immature Common Gull has brown in upperwing.

COMMON GULL   immature (1st winter) 16 in (41 cm) resident

Black in upperwings. Clear-cut black tail tip.

👁 Grey back with brown, grey and black upperwings. Clear-cut black tail tip.

★ Common, inland and coastal. First-year Herring and Black-backed Gulls have less distinct tail bands, no grey in mid-upperwings. Immature Black-headed Gull has white wedges in outer wings.

SANDWICH TERN   16 in (41 cm) summer visitor

Black cap. Black bill has yellow tip. Black legs.

👁 Forked tail. Black bill with yellow tip. (Crested early in breeding season.)

★ The largest tern, rather uncommon, nesting in specific coastal colonies. Beware – crest lost in mid-summer. Other summer terns with white underparts have red or yellow bills and legs.

STONE CURLEW   16 in (41 cm) summer visitor

Black mask. Wings prominently black, barred white. Black streaks on back.

◉ Oversized yellow eyes, and prominent eye stripes and wing bars.

★ A rare visitor to the south, nesting on barren open ground. A 'thick-knee' rather than a curlew; no confusion is likely with any other species. 'Freezing' and stilted movements are characteristic.

BLACK GROUSE   female 16 in (41 cm) resident

Very dark brown, appears black in poor light.

◉ Mostly dark brown with white-feathered legs. Long notched tail.

★ Uncommon, local to favoured sites, notably remote moorland and forest margins. Female Red Grouse is smaller, with stubby tail; female Capercaillie has orange throat, white on belly.

RAZORBILL   summer 16 in (41 cm) resident

Black bill, head, throat and all upperparts. Black legs.

◉ Glossy black. Broad 'razor' bill with white vertical stripe. Black cheeks.

★ Fairly common maritime species. Nests on remote coastal cliffs and islands. Black and ordinary Guillemots are similar, but note unmarked, pointed bills. Winter birds are white-cheeked.

RAZORBILL   winter 16 in (41 cm) resident

Black bill, crown, nape and all upperparts. Black legs.

◉ Broad black 'razor' bill with a white vertical stripe. White cheeks.

★ Fairly common but normally thoroughly maritime throughout winter months. Black and ordinary Guillemots are similar, but note unmarked, pointed bills. Summer birds are black-cheeked.

TUFTED DUCK   male 17 in (43 cm) resident

Black head, breast, upperparts and undertail.

◉ A crested duck, with brilliant white flanks (visible at great distances).

★ Widespread and common. Breeds at large freshwater locations. After breeding, becomes highly visible, even on park ponds. Female is brown-flanked. Male Goldeneye has cheek spot.

AVOCET   17 in (43 cm) resident and passage migrant

Black bill, cap, hindneck and wing tips. Transverse bands on back and wings.

👁 Long, strongly upturned bill.

★ Having been extinct in the British Isles, it is now a very scarce breeding species, restricted to some shallow lagoon sites in East Anglia. It is also a scarce coastal migrant.

OYSTERCATCHER   17 in (43 cm) resident

Black head, upper breast, upper back and tail tip. Black wings with bold bars.

👁 Pink legs, stout orange bill. Bold white rump and wing markings.

★ Quite common, breeds inland in north, otherwise on coasts. Noisy and highly visible. Noted ability to prise open shellfish. The mostly brown Redshank may confuse with similar markings in flight.

HEN HARRIER   male 17 in (43 cm) resident

Black wing tips. Dark trailing edges to wings.

👁 Low, slow, hunting flight. Grey tail and upperwings with a white rump.

★ Uncommon, with a northern and western breeding distribution. In winter visits fens, coasts and open country. Larger female, and both sexes of Marsh Harrier, have brown backs.

MAGPIE   18 in (46 cm) resident

Head, breast, upper back, blackest. Other 'black' is blue, green or brown!

👁 'Black' and white bird, with an extremely long, wedge-shaped tail.

★ Common and highly visible, but requires trees or at least bushes. Builds a remarkable football-shaped nest of twigs, very obvious in bare branches. Member of the crow family.

ROOK   18 in (46 cm) resident

Entirely black, except for bare face and base of bill.

👁 Entirely black, with greyish white bare face and base of bill.

★ Common and gregarious, nesting high in tops of large trees in 'rookeries', usually near farmland. Carrion Crow has black-feathered face, Hooded Crow has grey body. Jackdaw has grey nape.

ARCTIC SKUA   light phase 18 in (46 cm) passage migrant

Blackish cap. Whole bird may appear black and white only out at sea.

◗ Dark brown and white seabird, pointed central tail feathers projecting.

★ Uncommon migrant, but the commonest skua in British Isles, some breeding on Scottish moor and cliff sites. Dark-bodied phase rarer. Confusion with immature gulls a remote possibility.

POCHARD   male 18 in (46 cm) resident

Black breast, rump and tail. (Black extends up from breast around body.)

◗ Reddish brown head, black breast, grey back.

★ Not very common breeding species, but widespread, mostly on lakes. Winter migrants swell numbers at reservoirs, lakes, etc. Female mostly brownish. Female Goldeneye has grey breast.

GOLDENEYE   male 18 in (46 cm) winter visitor

Dark green head appears black with cheek spot. Black back, wing tips and tail.

◗ Dark (green) head has white face spot.

★ Uncommon. Seen both at sea and on fresh water, making prolonged dives. Female has plain brown head and similar inner wing. Male Tufted Duck crested, with clear-cut white flank panel.

HOODED CROW   18½ in (47 cm) resident

Black head, most of wings and tail.

◗ Medium-large size. Grey body with black wings.

★ Both Crows are very common, usually favouring open country with trees. Hooded Crow is found throughout Ireland, north and west Scotland. (Carrion Crow is the same species.)

CARRION CROW   18½ in (47 cm) resident

All black.

◗ Medium-large, entirely black bird (including face and all of bill).

★ Both Crows are very common, favouring open country with trees. (Ireland has the grey-bodied Hooded Crow only.) Rook has a whitish face. Jackdaw has grey nape. Raven calls 'prruk' and is far larger.

COMMON SCOTER   male 19 in (48 cm) winter visitor
Entirely black, except for patch on bill.

◉ Sea duck. Entirely black, except for yellowish patch on bill.

★ Rare breeding species, but common enough around British coasts in winter. Forms low-flying groups, only likely to be seen by sea-watching. Female is all brown.

GADWALL   male 20 in (51 cm) resident and winter visitor
Black in speculum. Black tail and undertail.

◉ Greyest-looking duck, with prominent white patch near sitting bird's tail.

★ Scarce breeding species, augmented by winter visitors. Prefers slow-moving fresh water. Brown female shows orange on bill, prominent in good light. Male Wigeon has yellow blaze on head.

BLACK GROUSE   male 21 in (53 cm) resident
Most of head, body, upperwings and tail is glossy blue-black.

◉ Robust black bird, with remarkable lyre-shaped tail and white wing bars.

★ Uncommon, restricted to favoured sites, notably remote moorland and forest margins. Males gather at courtship display areas called leks. Male Capercaillie has rounded tail.

LESSER BLACK-BACKED GULL   adult 21 in (53 cm) resident
Back and upperwings can be very dark; wing tips are black (white margins).

◉ Back and wings are dark grey (can vary in intensity); yellow legs.

★ Fairly common, breeds on level sites around coasts, but also inland. Pink-legged Herring Gull very similar to the palest Lessers. Much larger Great Black-backed also has pink legs.

EIDER   male 23 in (58 cm) resident
Black crown, flanks, belly and tail. Brown in wing looks black in flight.

◉ Sea duck, mostly white above, mostly black below. Pastel green on nape.

★ Common. Breeds round all northern coasts, lining nest with breast down. In winter, seen off all coasts. Late in year it turns dark ('eclipse' plumage). Goosander and Shelduck have green heads.

RED-BREASTED MERGANSER   male 23 in (58 cm) resident

Head very dark green. Black on back, wings, and 'scalloping' by breast.

👁 Green head shows double crest. White speculum and inner wing. 'Saw'-billed.

★ Rather uncommon. Breeds in north and west near water; includes sites far inland. Sea-going in winter. Male Goosander is white-bodied. Male Mallard has dark inner wing and blue speculum.

RED-BREASTED MERGANSER   female 23 in (58 cm) resident

Black wing tips.

👁 Chestnut head has double crest. Pale throat. White speculum. 'Saw'-billed.

★ Rather uncommon. Breeds in north and west near water; includes sites far inland. Sea-going in winter. Female Goosander has smoother crest, and dark neck contrasts with pale breast.

BRENT GOOSE   23 in (58 cm) winter visitor

Black head and neck, tail tip and legs. Upperparts and belly can look blackish.

👁 Smallest and darkest goose, with whole of head black.

★ Large, highly visible winter flocks gather at southerly estuarine and coastal field locations. Otherwise sea-going. Barnacle and Canada Geese are dark-necked, but have white on faces.

RED KITE   24 in (61 cm) resident

Black wing tips. Black in mid-wing carpal patch.

👁 Large soaring bird of prey, with angled wings and forked tail.

★ Currently scarce, restricted to Welsh wooded valleys (attempts to introduce elsewhere). Juvenile has darker outer wing patches. Buzzard has quite different wing patterns and proportions.

MUSCOVY DUCK   domestic 24 in (61 cm)

Very variable amounts of black areas, darkest 'wild' variation illustrated.

👁 Variable, the 'ugly' farmyard or village pond duck. A red knob on the bill.

★ Domesticated, a heavy-bodied duck mostly kept for the table. Originally from the Americas, not established in the wild in the British Isles. All Mallard strains are slimmer and possess tail curl.

RAVEN   25 in (64 cm) resident

All black.

◉ Large, entirely black bird. Call is a deep 'prruk'. Wedge-shaped tail.

★ Not at all common. Only found in west and north of region, mostly in remote areas with hills or cliffs. Aerobatic displays can be superb! Crows and Rooks are smaller with 'crar' or 'carr' calls.

BARNACLE GOOSE   25 in (64 cm) winter visitor

Black crown, neck, back, rump and tail tip. Black feather-edging in wings.

◉ Goose with white face and grey back.

★ Only common at favoured sites on north and west coastal grasslands, where they may gather in thousands. Canada Goose has white 'chinstrap'. Brent Goose has white neck patch. Both are brown-backed.

GOOSANDER   male 26 in (66 cm) resident

Black back, dark wing tips and green head. Bird may look black and white.

◉ Whitish overall, including breast. All of head dark green. 'Saw'-billed.

★ Rather uncommon. Northerly breeding, normally by fresh water. More widely spread in winter. Merganser, Mallard and Shoveler males have dark breast or flanks. Male Goldeneye has face spot.

PINTAIL   male 26 in (66 cm) winter visitor

Black on back, tail and undertail.

◉ Long pointed tail. 'Finger' of white rising from breast into dark head.

★ Mainly rather uncommon winter visitor to coasts and estuaries. Also a scarce breeding species. Some similarity to darker-breasted, yellow-crowned Wigeon, but only at long distances.

GREAT BLACK-BACKED GULL   adult 26 in (66 cm) resident

Back and wings very dark or black. Wing tips black with white margins.

◉ Black back and wings, pink legs. Great size alone is often sufficient.

★ Reasonably common, breeds on cliffs, but oddly absent from eastern coasts (not Ireland). More widespread in winter. Lesser Black-backed is smaller, greyer-backed, and has yellow legs.

BITTERN   30 in (76 cm) resident

Most of head and upperparts are a mix of brown and black markings.

👁 A large, brown heron-type bird. Remarkable booming call is absolutely distinctive.

★ Very scarce breeding species, limited to a small number of reed bed locations, mainly in East Anglia. Rarely seen, except in low flight over reeds, but frequent calls will locate.

SHAG   30 in (76 cm) resident

Plumage entirely dark glossy green, appears black at a distance.

👁 Dark glossy green seabird, often with a crest visible.

★ Fairly common, much more sea-going than the Cormorant. May appear uncommon in comparison. Does not venture inland. Cormorant is larger, browner and has a white face patch.

GREY HERON   35 in (89 cm) resident

Twin black crests, and stripe on throat. Black flight feathers.

👁 Extremely long neck (folded back in flight). Grey back.

★ Not numerically common at all, but a big bird, often out in the open and highly visible. Builds platform nests in tree tops, often in colonies (can get very noisy!). Bittern similar, but very brown.

CORMORANT   summer 36 in (91 cm) resident

Appears mostly black, although back and wings are really dark brown.

👁 Large dark seabird with a white face patch.

★ Fairly common and highly visible on most coasts. Nests on cliffs and small islands. Frequently seen at large bodies of inland water. Shag is wholly dark green and is sea-going all year round.

GANNET   adult 36 in (91 cm) resident

Black wing tips, visible at extreme distances. Black around eyes, chin.

👁 Sea-going. Long, 6 ft (2 m) wingspan, white wings, black-tipped. Dramatic diver.

★ A successful species, breeding in only about 20 off-shore gannetries around the British Isles. Mostly seen well out to sea, sometimes in lines. Adult plumage from fourth year.

GANNET   juvenile 36 in (91 cm) resident

Dark plumage lessens with age. Black in tail and wings, visible for 3 years.

● Sea-going. Long, 6 ft (2 m) wingspan, narrow wings with varying brown speckling.

★ A successful species, breeding in only about 20 off-shore gannetries around the British Isles. Mostly seen well out to sea, sometimes in lines. Often dives from considerable height.

CANADA GOOSE   38 in (97 cm) resident

Black neck and most of head. Black tail tip.

● Goose with a white 'chinstrap' about face and brown back.

★ An introduced species, now thriving in England, less common elsewhere. Breeds by water, from reservoirs to town ponds! Winters on grassland. Barnacle Goose is grey-backed, Brent is dark-headed.

BEWICK'S SWAN   48 in (122 cm) winter visitor

Bill about half black, junction with yellow rather rounded. Black legs.

● Shortest-necked, stocky swan. Bill half yellow (rather rounded border).

★ A scarce winter visitor, usually forming flocks at favoured water and grassland locations. Whooper Swan has a more extensive 'triangle' of yellow down bill. Mute Swan has a red bill.

WHOOPER SWAN   58 in (147 cm) winter visitor

Bill black at tip, yellow penetrating in triangular wedge. Black legs.

● Extensive 'triangle' of yellow down bill. A large, long-necked swan.

★ Quite uncommon, forming winter flocks at favoured water and grassland locations. Bewick's Swan's bill is half yellow, the border being rather rounded. Mute Swan has a red bill.

GOLDCREST 3½ in (9 cm) resident

Orangey yellow crown, the male having a markedly orange central band.

◉ Tiny, active bird (smallest in region), greenish with orange crown.

★ Widespread. Very common in coniferous woodland, also gardens and other woodland. Might just be confused with small warblers (no wing bars or crown stripes), or tits (whitish cheeks).

WILLOW WARBLER 4½ in (11 cm) summer visitor

Yellowish underparts. (Variable, can be very bright on autumn juveniles.)

◉ 'Clean' colours, no wing bar. Best identified by descending notes in song.

★ Abundant visitor. Widespread, found in any habitat with some ground cover. The Chiffchaff is similar but its 'dirtier' markings and 'chiff-chaff' song should separate them.

CHIFFCHAFF 4½ in (11 cm) summer visitor

Buffy yellow underparts (variable, strongest on young autumn birds).

◉ 'Dirty' colours, no wing bar. Song distinctive, two-note 'chiff-chaff'.

★ Very common, except in far north, requiring trees or scrub. Willow Warbler is similar, but its 'cleaner' markings and descending notes in song should separate them.

BLUE TIT 4½ in (11 cm) resident

Can vary quite a lot, but underparts usually a fairly pale yellow.

◉ Cobalt-blue crown.

★ Associated with almost any tree or bush, they are very common and very widespread. Beware confusion with Great Tit, which has black crown and black belly stripe.

SISKIN male 4½ in (11 cm) resident and winter visitor

Bright yellow breast, face, double wing bars, rump and outer tail feathers.

◉ Streaked black, green and yellow bird, with a black forehead and chin.

★ Fairly common winter visitor, notably at garden peanut bags. Small breeding populations in coniferous woodlands, especially in Scotland. Female is plainer-faced. Beware similarity to unstreaked Greenfinch.

SISKIN   female 4½ in (11 cm) resident and winter visitor

Pale yellow sides to breast. Brighter wing bars, rump and outer tail feathers.

👁 Streaked black, green and yellow bird, with plain chin and striped crown.

★ Fairly common winter visitor, notably at peanut bags. Breeds in coniferous woodland locally, especially in Scotland. Male has black forehead and chin. Beware similarity to unstreaked Greenfinch.

GOLDFINCH   adult 4¾ in (12 cm) resident

Broad, brilliant yellow wing bars. Bright red band on head pattern.

👁 Red, white and black head pattern.

★ Common and widespread (except in north Scotland), found on both open ground and in gardens. They love thistle seeds. Head pattern eliminates confusion with other species.

GOLDFINCH   juvenile 4¾ in (12 cm) resident

Broad yellow wing bars, perhaps not quite as striking as adult's.

👁 Single broad, brilliant yellow wing bars, with the head streaked brown.

★ Common and widespread (except in north Scotland), found on both open ground and in gardens. They love thistle seeds. The Siskin is similar, but shows double yellow wing bars and is clearly greenish.

REDPOLL   male (both adults similar) 5 in (13 cm) resident

👁 Crimson forehead, deep pink breast.

👁 Crimson forehead and black chin.

★ Reasonably common, but easy to miss. Often in large acrobatic flocks, they require trees, from heaths to conifer plantations. The adult male Linnet has a crimson forehead with a whitish chin.

WOOD WARBLER   5 in (13 cm) summer visitor

Chrome yellow breast, face and eyebrow stripe. Upperparts yellowish green.

👁 Bright yellow throat and breast, and pure white belly.

★ Widespread, but quite scarce. Not easily seen in its mature woodland home. Far more colourful than either Willow Warbler or Chiffchaff. Also has an unmistakable trilling song.

DARTFORD WARBLER   5 in (13 cm) resident
Breast and flanks dark wine-red.

◉ Underparts are a dark wine-red. Long tail is often cocked.

★ Very uncommon, only a few hundred birds being found in gorse-covered areas of southern England. Really a Mediterranean species, this is the very northern tip of its range.

STONECHAT   male 5 in (13 cm) resident
Deep orange breast.

◉ Entirely black head with prominent white neck patch.

★ Widely present, but with a markedly western distribution. A bird of open country, frequently seen atop a gorse bush. Female and juvenile are duller and more streaked, as Whinchat.

STONECHAT   female and juvenile 5 in (13 cm) resident
Rather 'dirty' orange breast.

◉ Streaked head and upperparts, small white wing patch.

★ Widely present, but markedly western distribution. A bird of open country, often atop a gorse bush. Male has prominent white neck patch. Whinchat has white edging at base of tail.

LINNET   male 5¼ in (13.5 cm) resident
Crimson forehead and breast.

◉ Crimson forehead and breast, in summer. White on wings and tail, all seasons.

★ Widespread and numerous in most open country habitats. Forms twittering flocks outside the breeding season. Redpoll has black chin; Chaffinch has double white wing bars.

LONG-TAILED TIT   5½ in (14 cm) resident
Outer back, rump, flanks and undertail are all pink.

◉ Tiny bird with pink in plumage, and a disproportionately long tail.

★ Almost never on ground, they require trees or bushes, even if sparse. Numerous and widespread, forming small flocks outside breeding season. (Beware some similarity to ground-loving Pied Wagtail.)

REDSTART   male 5½ in (14 cm) summer visitor

Orange-red breast, paler belly. Rump and outer tail feathers brownish red.

● Reddish brown tail, frequently flicked. Obvious white forehead.

★ Widespread, but local and not very common. Preferred habitats are mature woods, or more open country with good cover. A very distinctive bird, with no look-alikes.

REDSTART   female 5½ in (14 cm) summer visitor

Buffy red belly. Rump and outer tail feathers brownish red.

● Reddish tail. Rest of bird brown or brownish, with buffy underparts.

★ Widespread, but local and not very common. Prefers mature woods, or more open country with good cover. Black Redstart is greyer, Garden Warbler and female Blackcap have dark brown tails.

BLACK REDSTART   male 5½ in (14 cm) summer visitor

Rump and outer tail feathers are brownish red.

● Very dark plumage, with frequently flicked, reddish brown tail.

★ A rare breeding bird to the British Isles, it is a ground-loving species. Often nests in cities in old walls or buildings. The drab female is browner and lacks the white wing patch.

BLACK REDSTART   female 5½ in (14 cm) summer visitor

Rump and outer tail feathers are brownish red.

● Reddish tail. Rest of bird greyish brown, including underparts.

★ Rare breeding bird in the British Isles. A ground-loving species, often nesting in old walls or on buildings. Blackish male has white wing patch. Female Redstart has buffy underparts.

ROBIN   adult 5½ in (14 cm) resident

Orange-red extends from breast, right up to the forehead.

● Orange-red extends from breast, right up to the forehead.

★ Widespread and abundant in gardens and woodland everywhere. A gardener's 'friend' but bold and aggressive towards other birds. Male Stonechat and Redstart have black faces.

GREAT TIT   5½ in (14 cm) resident

Yellow breast and belly (divided by black stripe). Yellow nape patch.

👁 Black stripe from chin to belly (broader on male bird).

★ A very common bird, found wherever trees and hedgerows occur, and a familiar garden species. The smaller, blue-headed Blue Tit also has a belly stripe, but fainter and blue-grey.

NUTHATCH   5½ in (14 cm) resident

Buffy orange underparts, with brownish red on flanks.

👁 Climbs about tree trunks in any direction. Blue-grey upperparts.

★ Reasonably common throughout Wales and southern England, invariably associated with trunks of trees. Treecreeper shares habitat, but is mainly brown and only ascends trunks.

WHEATEAR   male 5¾ in (14.5 cm) summer visitor

Buffy orange chin and breast.

👁 Black inverted 'T' on the white tail. Grey crown and back.

★ Reasonably common, and very visible in western and northern regions. Likes wide open spaces – cliff tops, moors, bare uplands. Female and Whinchat have brown heads and backs.

WHEATEAR   female 5¾ in (14.5 cm) summer visitor

Buffy orange chin and breast, not quite as bright as male.

👁 Dark inverted 'T' on the white tail. Brown crown and back.

★ Reasonably common, and very visible in western and northern regions. Likes wide open spaces – cliff tops, moors and bare uplands. Male has grey back, Whinchat streaked back.

CHAFFINCH   male 5¾ in (14.5 cm) resident

Pinkish breast, flanks and face.

👁 Prominent white wing bars and tail feathers. Grey-blue crown on male bird.

★ A truly abundant bird, found on farms in flocks, in gardens, hedgerows and woodland. Female is brown-headed. Winter Brambling has white rump; other finches lack double wing bars.

GREENFINCH male 5¾ in (14.5 cm) resident

Bright yellow wing patches and outer tail. Mainly yellowish green.

👁 Yellowish green (intensity can vary), with bright yellow in wings and tail.

★ Very common and widespread in a variety of habitats, particularly gardens, woodland margins and arable fields. Female and juvenile are duller. Siskin is green and yellow, streaked.

GREENFINCH female and juvenile 5¾ in (14.5 cm) resident

Bright yellow wing patches and outer tail.

👁 Prominent yellow wing and tail flashes. Greenish brown head and back.

★ Very common and widespread in gardens and woodland margins. Male has green back and yellow flashes. Beware confusion with female House Sparrow (no wing markings); juvenile Goldfinch (yellow wing bar).

BULLFINCH male 5¾ in (14.5 cm) resident

Superb bold pink on face, throat and breast.

👁 White rump, bright pink breast.

★ Common and widespread, it is found in woods and gardens. Noted as an orchard pest due to its liking for buds. Female and juvenile are brown-breasted, the latter without the cap.

LESSER SPOTTED WOODPECKER 6 in (15 cm) resident

Bright red crown (absent on female). Face and underparts buff.

👁 White-barred back ('skeleton's bones'!). Male only has red crown.

★ Uncommon, restricted to southern Britain, and found in well-timbered habitats. Great Spotted Woodpecker is similar, but has obvious white 'shoulder-blades' and is nearly the size of a Blackbird.

BRAMBLING winter 6 in (15 cm) winter visitor

Breast, flanks and forewings are a striking orange.

👁 White rump, orange breast.

★ Rather uncommon, fluctuating numbers arrive from September onwards. Beech woods are a favourite location, but they are seen in open fields also. Chaffinch is similar, but has a green rump.

YELLOW WAGTAIL   6½ in (17 cm) summer visitor

All underparts yellow. Face and all upperparts are a greenish yellow.

◉ Repeated tail-wagging, combined with yellowish green back colouring.

★ Rather uncommon, preferring meadow and marshy breeding conditions, mostly restricted to England and Wales. Grey Wagtail is very yellow, but has grey face and extremely long tail.

YELLOWHAMMER   male 6½ in (17 cm) resident

Most of head and underparts yellow. Orangey partial breast bar and rump.

◉ Almost all of head yellow (brighter markings than female), brown back.

★ Common and widespread in most open habitats with bushy cover. Repetitive song is often rendered 'a little bit of bread and no che-ese'! Female Reed Bunting has brown and white head.

YELLOWHAMMER   female 6½ in (17 cm) resident

Underparts a rather dull, streaked yellow. Orangey brown rump.

◉ Almost all of head yellow (darker markings than male), brown back.

★ Common and widespread in most open habitats with bushy cover. Repetitive song is often rendered 'a little bit of bread and no che-ese'! Female Reed Bunting has brown and white head.

CROSSBILL   male 6½ in (17 cm) resident

Wings and tail apart, whole bird is brick-red (young males are more orange).

◉ Crossed bills. Mostly red, but tints may vary from dull to a strong brick-red.

★ Quite uncommon (continental birds may swell numbers periodically), almost invariably in coniferous forest. A similar separate species exists in Scotland. The female is yellowish green.

KINGFISHER   6½ in (17 cm) resident

Rich orange on face and underparts.

◉ Brilliant blue upperparts, rich orange underparts.

★ Fairly uncommon in most areas, and almost absent from Scotland. Prefers slow-moving water, streams or lakes, nesting in a nearby bank. Flashes by with remarkable whirring wing action.

GREY WAGTAIL   summer male 7 in (18 cm) resident
Brilliant yellow underparts and rump.

👁 Extreme length of tail, repeatedly wagged. Grey face, black throat.

★ Widespread, reasonably common. Almost always close to fast-running streams. Female and winter male white-throated. Yellow Wagtail has yellowish green back. Pied Wagtail, no yellow at all.

GREY WAGTAILS   summer female and both sexes in winter 7 in (18 cm) resident
Yellow on underparts varies, but rump and undertail remain bright yellow.

👁 Extreme length of tail, repeatedly wagged. Grey face, white throat.

★ Widespread, reasonably common. Almost always close to fast-running streams. Summer male has black throat. Yellow Wagtail has yellowish-green back. Pied Wagtail, no yellow at all.

WAXWING   7 in (18 cm) winter visitor
Yellow in wings and on tail tip. Red 'wax' in wings. Sienna undertail.

👁 Red 'wax' in inner wing, crest and yellow tail tip are all unmistakable.

★ A distinctly scarce visitor. Small groups turn up in variable numbers in unpredictable locations, almost always on berried bushes. Could just be mistaken for Starling in flight.

SWALLOW   7½ in (19 cm) summer visitor
Dark brick-red throat and forehead. Pinky-buff underparts (male darker).

👁 Red face. Long, forked tail.

★ Common and widespread in open country, often nests in farm buildings. Dark brown Swift has scythe-shaped wings; House Martin has white rump; Sand Martin has brown breast bar.

RINGED PLOVER   adult 7½ in (19 cm) resident
Leg colour can be yellow or orange-yellow.

👁 Complete black breast band. White wing bar obvious in flight.

★ Breeds widely around coasts. Also a common winter sight on estuaries. Juvenile bird has partial breast band. Little Ringed Plover lacks wing bar. Dunlin is only similar in flight.

REDWING   8 in (20 cm) winter visitor

Brick-red flanks, 'wingpits' and leading edge to underwings.

👁 Bold creamy eye stripe, brick-red flanks.

★ Numerous winter visitor, usually seen in flocks on open fields, or raiding berried bushes in gardens and hedges. Song Thrush, Mistle Thrush and winter Fieldfare all lack the eye stripe.

PURPLE SANDPIPER   winter 8½ in (22 cm) passage migrant and winter visitor

Yellow, or orange-yellow legs.

👁 A stout, dark bird of rocky coasts, with sooty head and dark back.

★ Rather uncommon, restricted to rocky coasts in winter, where it can be difficult to pick out. Much darker than Dunlin. Winter Turnstone has distinctive pied markings in flight.

GREAT SPOTTED WOODPECKER   9 in (23 cm) resident

Both sexes have brilliant crimson undertail, male has nape patch also.

👁 White 'shoulder' patches.

★ Widespread, it is the commonest British woodpecker. Dependent on trees and hedgerows. Lesser Spotted Woodpecker is similar, but uncommon and only sparrow-sized.

TURNSTONE   summer 9 in (23 cm) passage migrant

Rich, reddish brown markings on back and wings. Orange legs.

👁 'Tortoiseshell' back plumage, white on head.

★ Seen on passage around rocky coasts, usually very well-camouflaged. Summer dark-headed, dark-backed Purple Sandpiper should not confuse. Ringed Plover prefers sand and pebbles.

TURNSTONE   winter 9 in (23 cm) passage migrant and winter visitor

Orange legs.

👁 Dark head and breast. White back and double wing bar is distinctive in flight.

★ Does not breed in Britain, but is seen around rocky coasts, usually well-camouflaged. Some birds overwinter. Purple Sandpiper is very dark with a single wing bar visible in flight.

LITTLE TERN   9½ in (24 cm) summer visitor

Yellow bill with a black tip. Orange-yellow legs.

👁 Forked tail, and yellow bill with a black tip.

★ An uncommon and vulnerable seabird, breeding locally on shingle and sandy coasts. Small size distinctive, but note much larger Sandwich Tern's bill is black with a yellow tip.

FIELDFARE   10 in (25 cm) winter visitor

Beautiful golden-yellow breast (with black markings). Reddish brown back

👁 Grey head and tail, brown back.

★ A numerous winter visitor to Britain, favouring open country. It will raid gardens to strip berried bushes in hard winters. Mistle Thrush is similar but is grey-brown above.

LITTLE GREBE   summer 10¾ in (27 cm) resident

Chestnut-red cheeks and throat. Prominent yellow patch at bill base.

👁 'Sawn-off' fluffy tail. Chestnut cheeks and throat. Dives when disturbed.

★ Widespread and reasonably common, but very wary. Prefers quiet bodies of water, making it a difficult species to observe. Tail distinguishes it from all usual waterfowl at a glance.

TURTLE DOVE   10¾ in (27 cm) summer visitor

Rich orange 'scalloped' inner wings and outer back. Pink throat and breast.

👁 Neck patch. 'Scalloped' orange-brown outer back and inner wings.

★ Fairly common in the south and east, associated with trees and cultivated land. Song is a soft 'purring'. Collared Dove has a plain brown back and harsh song. Stock Dove has no white.

WATER RAIL   11 in (28 cm) resident

Long red bill. Creamy orange undertail.

👁 'Chicken-shaped' with long bill.

★ Uncommon, secretive and restricted to reed beds and marshy areas with cover. You could spend a lifetime just missing this bird! But a glimpse of its bill separates it from a Moorhen.

GOLDEN PLOVER   summer 11 in (28 cm) resident (the northern form is illustrated)

All upperparts except wing tips are a mixture of golden-brown and black.

◗ Varying amounts of black on belly; stubby bill; golden-brown upperparts.

★ Not very common, and easily missed on inaccessible, northerly upland moors. More visible on passage. Grey Plover is bulkier and silvery grey above. Ruff has white belly and divided white rump.

GOLDEN PLOVER   winter 11 in (28 cm) resident

Virtually all upperparts are golden-brown and black. Golden breast bar.

◗ Golden-brown upperparts, including rump. Wing bar is barely discernible.

★ Not very common, but highly visible in winter flocks on lowland fields, mainly in the south. Grey Plover is bulkier, silvery grey above. Winter Ruff has white belly, divided white rump.

REDSHANK   11 in (28 cm) resident

Long, orange-red legs. Bill orange with a black tip.

◗ Long red legs, obvious white 'triple triangle' flight markings above.

★ Common and widespread. Breeds on moors and marshy areas. Estuaries are best winter sites. Greenshank and Spotted Redshank lack wing markings. Black and white Oystercatcher, flight markings are similar.

SPARROWHAWK   male 11 in (28 cm) resident

Reddish barred underparts and front of underwings. Yellow legs.

◗ Barred brick-red underparts. Grey back.

★ Widespread, reasonably common with numbers increasing. Round-tipped wings for hunting in woodland with dashing flight. Larger female has brown breast bars and back. Kestrel hovers.

SPOTTED REDSHANK   summer 11 in (28 cm) passage migrant

Long red legs. Some red in lower bill.

◗ Body almost completely black.

★ Scarce, with summer plumage most visible on northerly migration in May. Seen on coasts, or marshy areas inland. Redshank and Greenshank are both much paler.

SPOTTED REDSHANK   winter 12 in (30 cm) passage migrant and winter visitor

Long red legs. Some red in lower bill.

👁 Long red legs, and white panel on back and rump (but not on wings).

★ Scarce, usually seen on coasts, or marshy areas inland. Confusion with brown-backed Redshank possible, but grey back will distinguish. Greenshank has greenish legs.

LAPWING   12 in (30 cm) resident

Orange undertail (prominent when feeding), buffy nape, reddish legs.

👁 Crest, and flapping flight.

★ Common and widespread, a familiar bird of farmland and open ground. 'Pee-wit' call gives the bird its country name. At a distance, golden-brown Golden Plover might appear similar.

PARTRIDGE   12 in (30 cm) resident

Orange-red face. Orange-brown flank stripes.

👁 'Chicken-shaped', with orange-red face, grey neck and breast.

★ Quite common on agricultural land, often in small groups (coveys). Nervous, disturbs easily. Red-legged Partridge has white face and black 'necklace'; Pheasant is long-tailed.

PUFFIN   summer 12 in (30 cm) resident

Bright orange legs and feet. Bill has yellow, orange and red sectors.

👁 Multi-coloured triangular bill. At a distance, note whirring wing action.

★ Fairly common, visiting off-shore islands to breed in summer. Bill distinguishes it from larger relatives, Razorbill and Guillemot. (Note that bill is smaller on winter adult and juvenile.)

GREEN WOODPECKER   12½ in (32 cm) resident

Crimson crown and moustache. Greenish yellow rump and underparts.

👁 Biggish green bird with a crimson crown. Laughing 'yaffle' call.

★ Common enough within southerly range, but completely absent from Ireland and much of Scotland. Very distinctive, often seen feeding on lawns, as well as in heath and woodland habitat.

135

HOBBY 13 in (33 cm) summer visitor
Brick-red thighs and undertail, yellow feet.

◉ Small bird of prey with pointed wings, red leggings and distinct moustache.

★ Very uncommon, breeding on southern heaths and open country. 'Hawks' agilely on insects and small birds. Robust adult Peregrine is similar, but barred grey below. Male Merlin has faint moustaches.

STOCK DOVE 13 in (33 cm) resident
Good views reveal a beautiful rose-red throat and breast. Red feet.

◉ Very plain bluish grey pigeon-type, with black upperwing borders.

★ Fairly common in many habitats, only absent in far north. Often overlooked with other pigeon-types. Woodpigeon has wing flashes. Feral Pigeon has black underwing borders and double wing bars.

'RED CHEQUER' FERAL PIGEON 13 in (33 cm) resident
Reddish brown and reddish grey tones dominate. Variable. Red feet.

◉ Reddish and pale grey tones on a pigeon-type.

★ Feral Pigeons are very varied (Chequers, black/white, Fantail, racing strains), widespread and common in towns and on fields. Rock Dove ancestors now only found on north and west coasts.

MOORHEN 13 in (33 cm) resident
Bright red frontal shield and bill base. Yellow bill tip. Yellow-green legs.

◉ White flank stripes, red frontal shield over bill.

★ Common and widespread where there are freshwater sites with cover. Easily alarmed; undertail flashes warning. Coot has white frontal shield and plain flanks. Water Rail has long bill.

COMMON TERN 13½ in (34 cm) summer visitor
Red bill with black tip. Red legs.

◉ Forked tail, black tip to red bill, black cap.

★ Only moderately common, but breeds by inland water as well as on coasts, so highly visible. Arctic Tern very alike, but whole bill is blood-red. Black-headed Gull has brown head!

BLACK GUILLEMOT   summer 13½ in (34 cm) resident

Bright red legs and feet.

👁 Pure white wing patch, red feet.

★ Locally fairly common, mainly around north and west coasts. Guillemot and Razorbill are plain dark above, but beware similarity to Eider in late summer plumage, seen at a distance out at sea.

RED-LEGGED PARTRIDGE   13½ in (34 cm) resident

Red bill and legs. Orange belly. Reddish undertail, outer tail and flank stripes.

👁 Chicken-like shape, black 'necklace'.

★ An introduced species, now locally common in south and east England on agricultural land. Partridge has an orange-red face. Female Pheasant is all brown with a long tail.

JAY   14 in (36 cm) resident

Nearly all of underparts, nape, back and forewings are brownish pink.

👁 Brilliant blue wing patches.

★ Common and widespread where there are trees; absent from far north. Quite shy, but bright colouring and raucous calls make this the most spectacular member of the crow family.

TEAL   male 14 in (36 cm) resident

Chestnut-red head. Spotted, pinkish breast. Yellowish undertail triangle.

👁 Chestnut head with dark green patch. Green and black speculum white-edged.

★ Widespread, rather uncommon breeding species, fond of rushy pools. Winter migrants swell numbers dramatically, forming groups on almost any body of water. Female is brown, with same speculum as male.

RED GROUSE   14 in (36 cm) resident

Almost entirely a rich, red-brown. Male with prominent red wattle over eye.

👁 Mostly red-brown with white-feathered legs. Male's red wattle prominent.

★ Normally associated with moorland and peat bogs, where they are common. Calls 'gobak-gobak-bak-bak'. Female Black Grouse is larger with longish, notched tail; Partridge is smaller farmland bird.

ARCTIC TERN   14½ in (37 cm) summer visitor

Blood-red bill, red legs.

👁 Forked tail, blood-red bill, black cap.

★ Fairly common, but mainly restricted to northern coastal breeding sites. Common Tern is very similar, but red bill has black tip. Black-headed Gull has brown head!

BLACK-HEADED GULL   summer 14½ in (37 cm) resident

Dark red bill and legs.

👁 Chocolate-brown 'hood' on head.

★ Common, the most visible inland gull. Breeds coastally, but also on inland marshy sites. Common and Arctic Terns are black-capped and have forked tails.

BLACK-HEADED GULL   winter 14½ in (37 cm) resident

Reddish bill, orange-red legs.

👁 Prominent white wedge in outer wing. Reddish legs and bill. White tail.

★ Common, the most visible inland gull. Happily associates with man, seen at parks, fields and water sites. Common Gull has yellow legs and bill. Herring Gull has pink legs, yellow bill.

BLACK-HEADED GULL   immature 14½ in (37 cm) resident

Dull orange bill and legs.

👁 Prominent white wedge in outer wing. Black band at tail tip.

★ Common, the most visible inland gull. Happily associates with man, seen at parks, fields and water sites. Immature Common and Herring Gulls have black tail tip, with all-dark outer wings.

CHOUGH   15 in (38 cm) resident

Bright red bill and legs. (Immature bird has orange bill.)

👁 All black, except for red bill and legs.

★ Scarcest of the crow family, having suffered a steady decline in numbers. Restricted to sea cliffs in west and south, commonest in Ireland. Bill distinguishes it from Jackdaw and Crow.

KITTIWAKE   adult 16 in (41 cm) resident

Plain yellow bill (shows a slightly greenish tinge).

☛ Yellow bill and black legs. 'Dipped-in-ink' wing tips seen in flight.

★ Perhaps surprisingly, the commonest British gull. Strictly maritime, it nests in colonies on cliffs, calling its name. Common Gull has yellow legs and white in wing tip.

COMMON GULL   adult 16 in (41 cm) resident

Unspotted yellow bill. Yellow legs. Both show a greenish tinge.

☛ Pale grey back, yellow legs. Note white within black wing tips.

★ Not the commonest gull, but common inland and coastally. Northerly breeding on moors, lochs and fields. Herring Gull has pink legs, Kittiwake black legs, and winter Black-headed Gull red legs.

SANDWICH TERN   16 in (41 cm) summer visitor

Black bill has a yellow tip.

☛ Forked tail. Black bill with yellow tip. (Crested early in breeding season.)

★ The largest tern, rathern uncommon, nesting in specific coastal colonies. Beware – crest lost in mid-summer. Other summer terns with white underparts have red or yellow bills and legs.

STONE CURLEW   16 in (41 cm) summer visitor

Yellow base to bill, oversized yellow eyes. Yellow legs.

☛ Oversized yellow eyes, and prominent eye stripes and wing bars.

★ A rare visitor to the south, nesting on barren open ground. A 'thick-knee' rather than a curlew; no confusion is likely with any other species. 'Freezing' and stilted movements are characteristic.

WOODPIGEON   16 in (41 cm) resident

Rose-red throat and breast. Red legs.

☛ Prominent white wing flashes visible in flight at considerable distances.

★ Abundant and widespread, usually near trees, although it feeds in open. Other pigeons and doves lack the white wing flashes, but Feral Pigeon and Stock Dove might confuse when seen at rest in fields.

139

OYSTERCATCHER   17 in (43 cm) resident
Orange bill, red eyes, pink legs.

👁 Pink legs, stout orange bill. Bold white rump and wing markings.

★ Quite common, breeds inland in north, otherwise on coasts. Noisy and highly visible. Noted ability to prise open shellfish. The mostly brown Redshank may confuse with similar markings in flight.

POCHARD   male 18 in (46 cm) resident
Chestnut-red head.

👁 Reddish brown head, black breast, grey back.

★ Not very common breeding species, but widespread, mostly on lakes. Winter migrants swell numbers at reservoirs, lakes, etc. Female mostly brownish. Female Goldeneye has grey breast.

WIGEON   male 18 in (46 cm) mainly a winter visitor
Orange-brown head with a buffy yellow crown stripe. Pink breast.

👁 Yellowish blaze down the crown and forehead. White inner forewing.

★ A common winter visitor, flocking on large water bodies, the sea and coastal grasslands. Also a passage migrant and scarce breeding species. Female Goldeneye has a white collar.

GREAT CRESTED GREBE   summer 19 in (48 cm) resident
Reddish orange in ear-tufts and on flanks. Red eyes, pale red bill.

👁 Dark crest and ear-tufts.

★ Much less common than might be expected, this species is highly visible and distinctive in summer on large bodies of open water. It is also widely seen at sea in winter.

SHOVELER   male 20 in (51 cm) resident and winter visitor
Bold chestnut flanks and belly.

👁 Remarkable spoon-like bill. Dark green head with white breast.

★ Uncommon breeding species, augmented by winter visitors. Prefers shallow water for dabbling, usually in small numbers. Female is brown. Mallard and Merganser males are brown-breasted.

BLACK GROUSE   male 21 in (53 cm) resident

Prominent red wattle (or 'comb') over the eyes, absent on female.

◉ Robust black bird, with remarkable lyre-shaped tail and white wing bars.

★ Uncommon, restricted to favoured sites, notably remote moorland and forest margins. Males gather at courtship display areas called leks. Male Capercaillie has rounded tail.

LESSER BLACK-BACKED GULL   adult 21 in (53 cm) resident

Yellow bill with red spot. Yellow legs.

◉ Back and wings are dark grey (can vary in intensity); yellow legs.

★ Fairly common, breeds on level sites around coasts, but also inland. Pink-legged Herring Gull very similar to the palest Lessers. Much larger Great Black-backed also has pink legs.

HERRING GULL   adult 22 in (56 cm) resident

Yellow bill with red spot. Pink legs.

◉ Light grey back and wings, pink legs.

★ Common around most coasts, breeds on cliffs and dunes, venturing inland more in winter. Common Gull and the palest Lesser Black-backed have yellowish legs; Kittiwake has black legs.

MARSH HARRIER   female 22 in (56 cm) variable status

Buffy yellow on head and forewings. Yellow legs.

◉ Low, slow hunting flight. Dark brown, with creamy buff head and forewings.

★ A very scarce species, with migrants and the small breeding population both being irregular in numbers. Male Marsh and Hen Harriers have grey in wings. Brown female Hen Harrier has white rump.

EIDER   male 23 in (58 cm) resident

Some yellow at base of greenish bill. Delicate pink wash on breast.

◉ Sea duck, mostly white above, mostly black below. Pastel green on nape.

★ Common. Breeds round all northern coasts, lining nest with breast down. In winter, seen off all coasts. Late in year it turns dark ('eclipse' plumage). Goosander and Shelduck have green heads.

RED-BREASTED MERGANSER   male 23 in (58 cm) resident

Rich, chestnut-red breast. Red bill and legs.

👁 Green head shows double crest. White speculum and inner wing. 'Saw'-billed.

★ Rather uncommon. Breeds in north and west near water; includes sites far inland. Sea-going in winter. Male Goosander is white-bodied. Male Mallard has dark inner wing and blue speculum.

RED-BREASTED MERGANSER   female 23 in (58 cm) resident

Chestnut-red head. Red bill and legs.

👁 Chestnut head has double crest. Pale throat. White speculum. 'Saw'-billed.

★ Rather uncommon. Breeds in north and west near water; includes sites far inland. Sea-going in winter. Female Goosander has smoother crest, and dark neck contrasts with pale breast.

SHELDUCK   adult 24 in (61 cm) resident

Bold red-brown band encircles body. Red bill, male's knobbed. Pink legs.

👁 Build is mid-way between duck and goose. Broad chestnut band encircles body.

★ Common and widespread around coasts, usually nesting in rabbit burrows. Very visible at estuaries. Male distinguished from female and immature by the bulbous knob at the base of the red bill.

SHELDUCK   juvenile 24 in (61 cm) resident

Pink bill and legs with just an early hint of red-brown body band to come.

👁 Build is mid-way between duck and goose. Imperfect chest band. White cheeks.

★ Common and widespread around coasts, often at estuaries. Both parents have much bolder chest bands and dark cheeks, the male having a bulbous knob at the base of the red bill.

RED KITE   24 in (61 cm) resident

Strongly red-brown body and forewings. Orange tail. Yellow legs.

👁 Large soaring bird of prey, with angled wings and forked tail.

★ Currently scarce, restricted to Welsh wooded valleys (attempts to introduce elsewhere). Juvenile has darker outer wing patches. Buzzard has quite different wing patterns and proportions.

MUSCOVY DUCK   domestic 24 in (61 cm)

Heavy red bill, with an enlarged knob at base.

◉ Variable, the 'ugly' farmyard or village pond duck. A red knob on the bill.

★ Domesticated, a heavy-bodied duck mostly kept for the table. Originally from the Americas, not established in the wild in the British Isles. All Mallard strains are slimmer and possess tail curl.

CAPERCAILLIE   female 24 in (61 cm) resident

Reddish brown crown and upperparts. Orange face and throat, also on tail.

◉ Reddish brown upperparts. Orange face and throat. Long tail is stubby.

★ Scarce, and local to woodland areas in Scottish central highlands. Male is mostly black. Female Black Grouse is all dark, with a notched tail, and Red Grouse is all dark with a short, stubby tail.

GOOSANDER   female 26 in (66 cm) resident

Chestnut-red head, red bill and creamy breast.

◉ Chestnut head, smooth crest obscure. Neck/breast contrast 'Saw'-billed

★ Rather uncommon. Northerly breeding, normally by fresh water. More widely spread in winter. Female Merganser is very similar, but note spiky double crest; pale throat lacks contrasts.

PINTAIL   male 26 in (66 cm) winter visitor

Obvious pale yellow patch just before tail.

◉ Long pointed tail. 'Finger' of white rising from breast into dark head.

★ Mainly rather uncommon winter visitor to coasts and estuaries. Also a scarce breeding species. Some similarity to darker-breasted, yellow-crowned Wigeon, but only at long distances.

GREAT BLACK-BACKED GULL   adult 26 in (66 cm)
resident

Yellow bill with red spot. Pink legs.

◉ Black back and wings, pink legs. Great size alone is often sufficient.

★ Reasonably common, breeds on cliffs, but oddly absent from eastern coasts (not Ireland). More widespread in winter. Lesser Black-backed is smaller, greyer-backed, and has yellow legs.

143

SHAG   30 in (76 cm) resident

Prominent yellow edges to base of bill (which is otherwise black).

◉ Dark glossy green seabird, often with a crest visible.

★ Fairly common, much more sea-going than the Cormorant. May appear uncommon in comparison. Does not venture inland. Cormorant is larger, browner and has a white face patch.

GREYLAG GOOSE   33 in (84 cm) resident

Plain orange bill, pink legs.

◉ Large grey-brown goose, with a plain orange bill and pink legs.

★ Uncommon breeding species, but winter numbers swollen by migrants. Often seen at marshes and wet grassland. Brent, Barnacle and Canada Geese all have black necks and bills.

CAPERCAILLIE   male 34 in (86 cm) resident

Prominent red wattle (or 'comb') over the eyes, absent on female.

◉ Very large, robust bird. Dark plumage and long, rounded tail are distinctive.

★ Scarce, and local to woodland areas in Scottish central highlands. Female is mostly brown with orange face. Male Black Grouse has extraordinary lyre-shaped tail and white wing bars.

PHEASANT   male 35 in (89 cm) resident

Red face wattle. Body and tail are usually red-brown or orange-brown.

◉ Extremely long tail and red face wattle.

★ Originally introduced from Asia as a 'game' bird, now very common wherever there is woodland, but mostly seen on farmland. Female is all brown, but duller, also with a long tail.

GREY HERON   35 in (89 cm) resident

Yellow dagger-like bill. (Bill can be red temporarily in breeding season.)

◉ Extremely long neck (folded back in flight). Grey back.

★ Not numerically common at all, but a big bird, often out in the open and highly visible. Builds platform nests in tree tops, often in colonies (can get very noisy!). Bittern similar, but very brown.

144

CORMORANT   summer 36 in (91 cm) resident

Hooked yellow bill. Yellow throat pouch (often not visible).

👁 Large dark seabird with a white face patch.

★ Fairly common and highly visible on most coasts. Nests on cliffs and small islands. Frequently seen at large bodies of inland water. Shag is wholly dark green and is sea-going all year round.

GANNET   adult 36 in (91 cm) resident

Beautiful pale golden-yellow head and neck.

👁 Sea-going. Long, 6 ft (2 m) wingspan, white wings, black-tipped. Dramatic diver.

★ A successful species, breeding in only about 20 off-shore gannetries around the British Isles. Mostly seen well out to sea, sometimes in lines. Adult plumage from fourth year.

BEWICK'S SWAN   48 in (122 cm) winter visitor

Bill half yellow (rather rounded border with black).

👁 Shortest-necked, stocky swan. Bill half yellow (rather rounded border).

★ A scarce winter visitor, usually forming flocks at favoured water and grassland locations. Whooper Swan has a more extensive 'triangle' of yellow down bill. Mute Swan has a red bill.

WHOOPER SWAN   58 in (147 cm) winter visitor

Extensive 'triangle' of yellow projects into black area of bill.

👁 Extensive 'triangle' of yellow down bill. A large, long-necked swan.

★ Quite uncommon, forming winter flocks at favoured water and grassland locations. Bewick's Swan's bill is half yellow, the border being rather rounded. Mute Swan has a red bill.

MUTE SWAN   adult 60 in (152 cm) resident

Red bill.

👁 Largest and heaviest bird of the region. Swan with a red bill.

★ Widespread, reasonably common, very, very visible. Builds a huge nest near slow-moving water. Male has large black knob at bill base. Whooper and Bewick's Swans have yellow in bills.

GOLDCREST   3½ in (9 cm) resident

Slightly 'dirty' olive-green nape, back, flanks, rump and tail.

👁 Tiny, active bird (smallest in region), greenish with orange crown.

★ Widespread. Very common in coniferous woodland, also gardens and other woodland. Might just be confused with small warblers (no wing bars or crown stripes), or tits (whitish cheeks).

WILLOW WARBLER   4¼ in (11 cm) summer visitor

Olive-green crown, nape, back, rump, wings and tail.

👁 'Clean' colours, no wing bar. Best identified by descending notes in song.

★ Abundant visitor. Widespread, found in any habitat with some ground cover. The Chiffchaff is similar but its 'dirtier' markings and 'chiff-chaff' song should separate them.

CHIFFCHAFF   4¼ in (11 cm) summer visitor

Brownish olive-green crown, nape, back, rump, wings and tail.

👁 'Dirty' colours, no wing bar. Song distinctive, two-note 'chiff-chaff'.

★ Very common, except in far north, requiring trees or scrub. Willow Warbler is similar, but its 'cleaner' markings and descending notes in song should separate them.

BLUE TIT   4¼ in (11 cm) resident

Yellowish green nape, back and rump. Cobalt-blue crown, wings and tail.

👁 Cobalt-blue crown.

★ Associated with almost any tree or bush, they are very common and very widespread. Beware confusion with Great Tit, which has black crown and black belly stripe.

SISKIN   male 4¼ in (11 cm) resident and winter visitor

Yellow-green crown, nape, forewing and back. Greenish tinge to yellow parts.

👁 Streaked black, green and yellow bird, with a black forehead and chin.

★ Fairly common winter visitor, notably at garden peanut bags. Small breeding populations in coniferous woodlands, especially in Scotland. Female is plainer-faced. Beware similarity to unstreaked Greenfinch.

SISKIN   female 4½ in (11 cm) resident and winter visitor

Dull yellow-green upperparts and forehead. Yellow parts tinged with green.

◉ Streaked black, green and yellow bird, with plain chin and striped crown.

★ Fairly common winter visitor, notably at peanut bags. Breeds in coniferous woodland locally, especially in Scotland. Male has black forehead and chin. Beware similarity to unstreaked Greenfinch.

WOOD WARBLER   5 in (13 cm) summer visitor

'Clean' yellow green upperparts and eye stripe.

◉ Bright yellow throat and breast, and pure white belly.

★ Widespread, but quite scarce. Not easily seen in its mature woodland home. Far more colourful than either Willow Warbler or Chiffchaff. Also has an unmistakable trilling song.

GREAT TIT   5½ in (14 cm) resident

Yellowish green back. Forewings, rump and tail are grey-blue.

◉ Black stripe from chin to belly (broader on male bird).

★ A very common bird, found wherever trees and hedgerows occur, and a familiar garden species. The smaller, blue-headed Blue Tit also has a belly stripe; but fainter and blue-grey.

NUTHATCH   5½ in (14 cm) resident

Greyish blue upperparts.

◉ Climbs about tree trunks in any direction. Blue-grey upperparts.

★ Reasonably common throughout Wales and southern England, invariably associated with trunks of trees. Treecreeper shares habitat, but is mainly brown and only ascends trunks.

CHAFFINCH   male 5¾ in (14.5 cm) resident

Pale grey-blue crown, nape and outer back. Yellowish green rump.

◉ Prominent white wing bars and tail feathers. Grey-blue crown on male bird.

★ A truly abundant bird, found on farms in flocks, in gardens, hedgerows and woodland. Female is brown-headed. Winter Brambling has white rump; other finches lack double wing bars.

147

CHAFFINCH female and juvenile 5¾ in (14.5 cm) resident

Brownish green crown and back. Yellowish green rump.

◕ Prominent white wing bars and tail feathers. Green-brown head, and green rump.

★ A truly abundant bird, found in flocks on farms, in gardens, hedgerows and woodland. Male has grey-blue crown. Winter Brambling has white rump; other finches lack double wing bars.

GREENFINCH male 5¾ in (14.5 cm) resident

Mainly yellowish green, rather darker above.

◕ Yellowish green (intensity can vary), with bright yellow in wings and tail.

★ Very common and widespread in a variety of habitats, particularly gardens, woodland margins and arable fields. Female and juvenile are duller. Siskin is green and yellow, streaked.

YELLOW WAGTAIL 6½ in (17 cm) summer visitor

Yellowish olive-green upperparts.

◕ Repeated tail-wagging, combined with yellowish green back colouring.

★ Rather uncommon, preferring meadow and marshy breeding conditions, mostly restricted to England and Wales. Grey Wagtail is very yellow, but has grey face and extremely long tail.

CROSSBILL female 6¼ in (17 cm) resident

Yellowish green, except for wings and tail. Young birds greyer.

◕ Crossed bills. Mostly yellowish green. Young birds are greyer.

★ Quite uncommon (continental birds may swell numbers periodically), almost invariably in coniferous forest. A similar separate species exists in Scotland. Male red, but intensity varies.

KINGFISHER 6½ in (17 cm) resident

Most upperparts are brilliant blue or blue-green, back and rump pale blue.

◕ Brilliant blue upperparts, rich orange underparts.

★ Fairly uncommon in most areas, and almost absent from Scotland. Prefers slow-moving water, streams or lakes, nesting in a nearby bank. Flashes by with remarkable whirring wing action.

SWALLOW   7½ in (19 cm) summer visitor

Very dark blue upperparts and collar.

👁 Red face. Long, forked tail.

★ Common and widespread in open country, often nests in farm buildings. Dark brown Swift has scythe-shaped wings; House Martin has white rump; Sand Martin has brown breast bar.

STARLING   adult 8½ in (22 cm) resident

Glossy summer plumage shows greens, blues and purples in good light.

👁 Glossy summer plumage (speckled in winter). Pointed wings seen in flight.

★ Abundant. Forms huge noisy flocks before roosting in cities or country cover. Juvenile birds are a plain 'mouse-brown'. Not likely to be confused with any other common bird.

MERLIN   male 10¾ in (27 cm) resident

Blue-grey upperparts.

👁 Small bird of prey; pointed wings. Blue-grey above; faint moustache.

★ Uncommon. Favours upland, boggy and coast areas in north and west. Pursues prey with low-level dashing flight. Larger female is brown. Male Peregrine and Hobby have black heads and heavy moustaches.

GREENSHANK   12 in (30 cm) summer visitor and passage migrant

Legs visibly grey-green, bill less so.

👁 Long grey-green legs. Bill slightly upturned. White back 'V' in flight.

★ Uncommon breeding species in northern Scotland only. Mostly seen on passage at coasts, or inland water. More grey than the brown-backed Redshank. Beware similarity to red-legged winter Spotted Redshank.

LAPWING   12 in (30 cm) resident

'Black' upperparts are mainly a blend of dark green colours.

👁 Crest, and flapping flight.

★ Common and widespread, a familiar bird of farmland and open ground. 'Pee-wit' call gives the bird its country name. At a distance, golden-brown Golden Plover might appear similar.

GREEN WOODPECKER 12½ in (32 cm) resident

Back and wings are yellowish green. Rump and underparts greenish yellow.

◉ Biggish green bird with a crimson crown. Laughing 'yaffle' call.

★ Common enough within southerly range, but completely absent from Ireland and much of Scotland. Very distinctive, often seen feeding on lawns, as well as in heath and woodland habitat.

STOCK DOVE 13 in (33 cm) resident

Notably blue-grey in strong light. Vivid emerald-green neck patch.

◉ Very plain bluish grey pigeon-type, with black upperwing borders.

★ Fairly common in many habitats, only absent in far north. Often overlooked with other pigeon-types. Woodpigeon has wing flashes. Feral Pigeon has black underwing borders and double wing bars.

JAY 14 in (36 cm) resident

Brilliant blue wing patches.

◉ Brilliant blue wing patches.

★ Common and widespread where there are trees; absent from far north. Quite shy, but bright colouring and raucous calls make this the most spectacular member of the crow family.

TEAL male 14 in (36 cm) resident

Dark green 'tear-drop' patch about the eye, prominent green in speculum.

◉ Chestnut head with dark green patch. Green and black speculum white-edged.

★ Widespread, rather uncommon breeding species, fond of rushy pools. Winter migrants swell numbers dramatically, forming groups on almost any body of water. Female is brown, with same speculum as male.

TEAL female 14 in (36 cm) resident

Prominent green in speculum.

◉ Brown. Small size obvious in flight. Green and black speculum white-edged.

★ Widespread, rather uncommon breeding species, fond of rushy pools. Winter migrants swell numbers dramatically; groups may form at any body of water. Other ducks are larger, note speculums.

RUDDY DUCK   male 15 in (38 cm) resident

Bright, pale blue bill.

👁 A small duck with an upright, stiff tail and a bright blue bill.

★ A North American species added to British list in 1971, when wild populations became established. Still scarce, but regular at some lakes and reservoirs. Female more grey-brown.

PEREGRINE   male and female 15 in (38 cm) and 19 in (48 cm) respectively, resident

All upperparts are blue-grey.

👁 Pointed wings, bold black moustaches. Incredible 'stooping' dive on to prey.

★ Was endangered, still uncommon. Robust falcon, with female larger than male. Juvenile is brown. Breeds on cliffs, inland or coastal. Hobby and Merlin more agile and delicate. Kestrel hovers.

AVOCET   17 in (43 cm) resident and passage migrant

Bluish grey legs.

👁 Long, strongly upturned bill.

★ Having been extinct in the British Isles, it is now a very scarce breeding species, restricted to some shallow lagoon sites in East Anglia. It is also a scarce coastal migrant.

GOLDENEYE   male 18 in (46 cm) winter visitor

Dark green head (with white spot).

👁 Dark (green) head has white face spot.

★ Uncommon. Seen both at sea and on fresh water, making prolonged dives. Female has plain brown head and similar inner wing. Male Tufted Duck crested, with clear-cut white flank panel.

WIGEON   female 18 in (46 cm) mainly a winter visitor

Dark green speculum.

👁 Compact duck, reddish brown overall. Short, bluish, black-tipped bill.

★ A common winter visitor, flocking on large water bodies, the sea and coastal grasslands. Also passage migrant and scarce breeding species. Most plain ducks are darker-bellied (not Gadwall).

SHOVELER   male 20 in (51 cm) resident and winter visitor

Glossy dark green head, dark green in speculum. Pale blue forewing.

● Remarkable spoon-like bill. Dark green head with white breast.

★ Uncommon breding species, augmented by winter visitors. Prefers shallow water for dabbling, usually in small numbers. Female is brown. Mallard and Merganser males are brown-breasted.

SHOVELER   female 20 in (51 cm) resident and winter visitor

Dark green in speculum. Pale blue forewing less distinct than male's.

● Remarkable spoon-like bill, brown body. Pale blue inner wing in flight.

★ Uncommon breeding species, augmented by winter visitors. Prefers shallow water for dabbling, often solitary. Drake has dark head and white breast. Other similar ducks have dark inner wings.

MALLARD   male 23 in (58 cm) resident

Glossy dark green head. Blue (can be purplish) speculum.

● Blue (can be purplish) speculum. Tail curl. Green head and brown breast.

★ Commonest duck, widespread. Strains and intermediates can confuse, but speculum remains definitive. Male Shoveler has white breast. Male Red-breasted Merganser has white speculum.

MALLARD   female 23 in (58 cm) resident

Blue (can be purplish) speculum.

● Blue (can be purplish) speculum with white margins. Whole body brown.

★ Commonest duck, widespread. Many female duck species are mainly brown, but most have white belly; no other has blue speculum. Beware similarity to Pintail, Gadwall, Shoveler and Teal.

EIDER   male 23 in (58 cm) resident

Yellowish green bill. Pastel green on cheek and nape.

● Sea duck, mostly white above, mostly black below. Pastel green on nape.

★ Common. Breeds round all northern coasts, lining nest with breast down. In winter, seen off all coasts. Late in year it turns dark ('eclipse' plumage). Goosander and Shelduck have green heads.

RED-BREASTED MERGANSER   male 23 in (58 cm)
resident

Dark green head.

👁 Green head shows double crest. White speculum and inner wing. 'Saw'-billed.

★ Rather uncommon. Breeds in north and west near water; includes sites far inland. Sea-going in winter. Male Goosander is white-bodied. Male Mallard has dark inner wing and blue speculum.

SHELDUCK   adult 24 in (61 cm) resident

Glossy dark green head and neck. Green in speculum.

👁 Build is mid-way between duck and goose. Broad chestnut band encircles body.

★ Common and widespread around coasts, usually nesting in rabbit burrows. Very visible at estuaries. Male distinguished from female and immature by the bulbous knob at the base of the red bill.

GOOSANDER   male 26 in (66 cm) resident

Glossy dark green head.

👁 Whitish overall, including breast. All of head dark green. 'Saw'-billed.

★ Rather uncommon. Northerly breeding, normally by fresh water. More widely spread in winter. Merganser, Mallard and Shoveler males have dark breast or flanks. Male Goldeneye has face spot.

SHAG   30 in (76 cm) resident

Plumage overall is a glossy dark green.

👁 Dark glossy green seabird, often with a crest visible.

★ Fairly common, much more sea-going than the Cormorant. May appear uncommon in comparison. Does not venture inland. Cormorant is larger, browner and has a white face patch.

PHEASANT   male 35 in (89 cm) resident

Glossy green head (with red face wattle).

👁 Extremely long tail and red face wattle.

★ Originally introduced from Asia as a 'game' bird, now very common wherever there is woodland, but mostly seen on farmland. Female is all brown, but duller, also with a long tail.

GLOSSARY OF TERMS

Adult A mature bird, capable of breeding.

Band Broad strip of colour, across area described, e.g. tail of female Hen Harrier.

Bar Narrow strip of colour, across area described, e.g. body of Sparrowhawk.

Call Note, or limited number of notes. Either indicates alarm or acts as a statement of prescence.

Carpal patch Dark mid-wing mark, mostly on owls or birds of prey, e.g. Short-eared Owl, Buzzard.

Domestic Kept in captivity, no sustained breeding in the wild, e.g. Muscovy Duck.

Eclipse Dull plumage taken on by male ducks following post-breeding moult, e.g. Eider.

Feral Originally domestic stock, but now established in the wild, e.g. Feral Pigeon.

Flash Band of bright colour, usually on wings, e.g. Woodpigeon.

Form Term for plumage variation, often associated with a specific sub-species, e.g. Golden Plover.

Frontal shield Featherless structure on forehead of some water birds, e.g. Moorhen.

Game Term referring to birds traditionally shot for eating, e.g. Pheasant.

Hawking Manner of pursuit flight of agile birds of prey, e.g. Hobby.

Immature Describes birds which are full-sized but not yet capable of breeding, usually with their own plumage variation, e.g. gulls.

Juvenile A young bird, out of the nest, but still in its first plumage variation, e.g. Robin.

Nocturnal Normally active at night, e.g. Long-eared Owl.

Passage migrant Migratory species seen 'on passage', usually in spring or autumn, moving between summer and winter grounds, e.g. Ruff.

Patch A relatively large area of colour, e.g. on wing of Linnet.

Phase Alternative term for form, e.g. Arctic Skua.

Range The geographical area in which the great majority of a species is normally to be found.

Resident Present in an area throughout the year, even if this involves population movements, in and out during migration, e.g. Blackbird.

Roost Safe location where a bird sleeps.

Saw-bills A group of duck types with thin serrated bills, e.g. Goosander.

Scalloping Plumage pattern produced when feather edges and feather centres are different colours, e.g. Turtle Dove.

Song A sustained and consistent collection of notes, typical of the species, which proclaims ownership of territory, particularly during the breeding season.

Species A population of individuals, whose members resemble each other more closely than any other population, and almost invariably are capable of breeding only among themselves.

Speculum A panel on the trailing innerwing of ducks, usually distinctively coloured, e.g. Mallard.

Strain Variation, usually in plumage, of domesticated stock, e.g. racing pigeon.

Stoop Spectacular high-speed dive of Peregrine on to prey.

Stripe Narrow colour strip, along area described, e.g. crown of Whimbrel.

Sub-species A group within a species' population, which shows some plumage variation from the normal but which remains capable of interbreeding with other members of the population, e.g. Yellow Wagtail.

Summer visitor A migratory species arriving in spring and returning to its winter home after summer breeding in this region, e.g. Nightingale.

Tube-nosed Having raised nostrils within the bill structure, e.g. Fulmar.

Wader Broad term including a number of coastline and estuary species, mostly long-legged (for wading), and often highly migratory, e.g. Dunlin.

'Wingpits' Colloquial – we have armpits, birds have wingpits, e.g. Grey Plover.

Winter visitor A migratory species. arriving from autumn onwards. wintering in region. returning to breeding grounds in spring. e.g. Redwing.

BIBLIOGRAPHY

Useful 'next-level-up' field guides and reference works

Ferguson-Lees, J., Willis, I. and Sharrock, J. T. R. *The Shell Guide to Birds of Britain and Ireland*, Michael Joseph, 1983

Gooders, J. *Field Guide to the Birds of Britain and Ireland*, Kingfisher, 1988

Hayman, P. and Burton, P. *The Birdlife of Britain and Europe*, Mitchell Beazley, 1986

Heinzel, H., Fitter, R. and Parslow J. *The Birds of Britain and Europe with North Africa and the Middle East*, Collins, 1972

Hollom, P. A. D. *The Popular Handbook of British Birds*, (3rd edn.) Witherby, 1962

Peterson, R., Mountfort, G. and Hollom, P. A. D. *A Field Guide to the Birds of Britain and Europe*, Collins, 1954

Specialist guides

Brown, R., Ferguson, J., Lawrence, M. and Lees, D. *Tracks and Signs of the Birds of Britain and Europe. An Identification Guide*, Helm, 1987

Cramp, S. *et al. Handbook of the Birds of Europe, the Middle East and North Africa – The Birds of the Western Palaearctic*, Oxford University Press, 1977

Field Guide to the Birds of North America, National Geographic Society, 1983

Harris, A., Tucker, L. and Vinicombe, K *The Macmillan Field Guide to Bird Identification*, Macmillan, 1989

Harrison, P. *Seabirds: An Identification Guide*, (revised edn.) Helm, 1985

Hayman, P., Marchant, J. and Prater, T. *Shorebirds: An Identification Guide to the Waders of the World*, Helm, 1986

Madge, S. and Burn, H. *Wildfowl: An Identification Guide to the Ducks, Geese and Swans of the World*, Helm, 1988

Sharrock, J. T. R. *The Atlas of Breeding Birds in Britain and Ireland*, T. and A. D. Poyser, 1977

INDEX

Species						
Fulmar		72	94			
Gadwall, male		72	95	119		
female	35	73				
Gannet, adult		79		122	145	
juvenile	41	79		123		
Godwit, Bar-tailed winter	31	66	91	114		
Black-tailed, winter	32	67	91	115		
Goldcrest				98	124	146
Goldeneye, male		71		118		151
female	34	71	94			
Goldfinch, adult	11	43		99	125	
juvenile	11			99	125	
Goosander, male		77		121		153
female		77	96		143	
Goose, Barnacle		77	96	121		
Brent	38	76	96	120		
Canada	41	79		123		
Greylag	39		96		144	
Grebe, Great Crested, summer	34	72			140	
winter	34	72				
Little, summer	25				133	
winter	25	58				
Greenfinch, male					129	148
female and juvenile	17				129	
Greenshank		61	87			149
Grouse, Black male		73		119	141	
female	32			116		
Red	30				137	
Guillemot, summer	33	69				
winter	33	69				
Black, summer		63		112	137	
Gull, Black-headed, summer	30	65	90		138	
winter		65	91		138	
immature	30	65	91	113	138	
Common, adult		67	92		139	
immature (1st winter)	32	68	92	115		
Great Black-backed, adult		78		121	143	
immature (1st winter)	39	78				
Herring, adult		74	95		141	
immature (1st winter)	36	74				
Lesser Black-backed, adult		73	95	119	141	
immature (1st winter)	36	74				
Harrier, Hen, male		70	93	117		
female	35	73				
Marsh, male	35		94			
female	37				141	
Hawfinch	21	53		106		
Heron, Grey		78	97	122	144	
Hobby		62	88	110	136	
Jackdaw			89	111		
Jay		64		113	137	150
Kestrel, male	28	62	88	111		
female	29	64		112		

Kingfisher					130	148
Kite, Red	38	77		120	142	
Kittiwake, adult		67	92	115	139	
juvenile		67	92	115		
Knot, winter		58	86			
Lapwing		61		110	135	149
Linnet, male	13	46			126	
female and juvenile	14	46				
Magpie		70		117		
Mallard, male	37	75				152
female	37	75				152
Martin, House		45		100		
Sand	11	43				
Merganser, Red-breasted, male		76	95	120	142	153
female		76	95	120	142	
Merlin, male	26		86			149
female	28	62				
Moorhen	28	63		111	136	
Nightingale	20		84			
Nightjar	26	58				
Nuthatch			82	102	128	147
Osprey	37	75				
Ouzel, Ring, male		57		108		
female	24	57				
Owl, Barn	29	64				
Little	23	55				
Long-eared	29	64				
Short-eared	31	67		114		
Tawny	31					
Oystercatcher		70		117	140	
Partridge	27		88		135	
Red-legged	28	64	90	112	137	
Peregrine, male and female		66	91	114		151
juvenile	31			114		
Pheasant, male	40				144	153
female	36					
Pigeon, Feral/Rock Dove		63	89	111		
'Red Chequer'			89		136	
Pintail, male	39	78	96	121	143	
female	36					
Pipit, Meadow	18	50				
Rock	19		83			
Tree	18	50				
Plover, Golden, summer	26	59		109	134	
winter	27	59			134	
Grey, summer		59	87	109		
winter		60	87	109		
Little Ringed	19	50		104		
Ringed, adult	22	54		106	131	
juvenile	22	54				
Pochard, male			93	118	140	
female	33		93			
Puffin, summer		61		110	135	

Rail, Water	26	59	86		133	
Raven				121		
Razorbill, summer		69		116		
winter		69		116		
Redpoll, male	11	43		99	125	
Redshank	27	60			134	
Spotted, summer		60		109	134	
winter		60	87		135	
Redstart, male	15	47	82	101	127	
female	15				127	
Black, male		47		101	127	
female	15				127	
Redwing	23	55			132	
Robin, adult	15				127	
juvenile	16					
Rook		71	93	117		
Ruff, summer male	27	61		110		
female and winter male	24	57		107		
Sanderling, winter		55	85	106		
Sandpiper, Common	22	55				
Green		56		107		
Purple, winter		55	85		132	
Scoter, Common, male				119		
female	34					
Shag				122	144	153
Shearwater, Manx			65	113		
Shelduck, adult	38	76			142	153
juvenile	38	76			142	
Shoveler, male	35	73			140	152
female	35					152
Siskin, male		43		99	124	146
female		43		99	125	147
Skylark	21	53				
Skua, Arctic, light phase	33	71		118		
Snipe	25	58		108		
Sparrow, House, male	16		82	102		
female and juvenile	17					
Tree	16	48		102		
Sparrowhawk, male		60	87		134	
female	31	66				
Starling, adult	23			107		149
juvenile	23					
Stint, Little, juvenile	13	46		100		
Stonechat, male	13	45		100	126	
female and juvenile	13	45			126	
Swallow		54			131	149
Swan, Bewick's		79		123	145	
Mute, adult		80			145	
juvenile	41	80	97			
Whooper		80		123	145	
Swift				104		
Teal, male	29		90		137	150
female	30					150

Tern, Arctic		65	90	113	138	
Black, summer			85	108		
Common		63	90	112	136	
Little		57	85	108	133	
Sandwich		68	92	115	139	
Thrush, Mistle	25	58	86			
Song	23	56				
Tit, Bearded, male	19	51	83	104		
female	19	51				
Blue		42			124	146
Coal		42	81	98		
Crested	10	42		98		
Great		48		101	128	147
Long-tailed		46		101	126	
Marsh	10	42		98		
Willow	11	42		98		
Treecreeper	12	44				
Turnstone, summer	24	56		107	132	
winter	24	56			132	
Wagtail, Grey, summer male		52	84	105	131	
summer female and all winter		53	84	105	131	
Pied, summer male		52		105		
summer female and all winter		52	84	105		
juvenile	21	52	84	105		
Yellow		51		104	130	148
Warbler, Dartford	12		81		126	
Garden	16					
Reed	12	44				
Sedge	12	44		100		
Willow	10				124	146
Wood		44			125	147
Waxwing	22			106	131	
Wheatear, male		48	82	102	128	
female	17	48		102	128	
Whimbrel	32	68				
Whinchat	12	44				
Whitethroat, male	14	47	81			
female and juvenile	14	47				
Lesser	14	46	81			
Wigeon, male		71	94		140	
female	34	72				151
Woodcock	29			112		
Woodpecker, Green					135	150
Lesser Spotted		49		103	129	
Great Spotted		56		107	132	
Woodpigeon		68	93		139	
Wren	10					
Yellowhammer, male	19	51			130	
female	20	51			130